SQUASH

CROWOOD SPORTS GUIDES

SQUASH

TECHNIQUE • TACTICS • TRAINING

Eric Sommers

The Crowood Press

First published in 1991 by
The Crowood Press Ltd
Ramsbury, Marlborough
Wiltshire SN8 2HR

British Library Cataloguing in Publication Data

Sommers, Eric
  Squash: technique, tactics, training.
  1. Squash rackets
  I. Title
  796.343

ISBN 1 85223 543 8

Acknowledgements

I should like to thank Stephen Line for the excellent photographs and Jenny Hart for the instructional sketches which appear throughout this book.
  Thanks are also due to the Gatwick Penta Hotel for allowing us to use their courts to photograph the instructional pictures, and to Hiddy Jahan and Helen McFie for appearing alongside Eric Sommers in those pictures.
  Artwork by Taurus Graphics.

Throughout this book, the pronouns, 'he', 'him' and 'his' are used inclusively and are intended to apply to both males and females.

Typeset by Chippendale Type Ltd., Otley, West Yorkshire.
Printed in Hong Kong by South China Printing Co.

CONTENTS

FOREWORD

Eric Sommers chose to devote his days to the coaching of others at a time when he had the touch and the talent to have become a good tournament player. It was a decision for which many thousands of pupils have good cause to be grateful, for he has proved to be an exceptional coach.

Unlike so many of his counterparts, he has never been content simply to teach the bare rudiments of stroke play. Instead he has always sought the deeper secrets of squash and treated it quite rightly as physical chess.

He has encouraged his pupils to be positive and adventurous — and that too is admirable. Possibly the most pleasing feature of all is that the pleasure which he so clearly gains from the game has been passed on to all those around him.

Recently he has taken time out from his coaching to win the European Over-35 Squash Championship and also the British Racketball Championship. I consider Eric a credit to the game and heartily recommend his book.

Hiddy Jahan

PREFACE

This book has been designed to help players (of all standards) to improve their performances.

For *beginners*, this is a step-by-step guide to take you from the novice stage to that of experienced campaigner. Be patient. Read slowly. Pick up a racket and practise as you go. The chapters are arranged in the logical sequence to suit your progression, so make sure you understand one phase before you move on to the next. Above all else, do not be in too much of a hurry. First, get the basic habits right, and then build your game upon them.

For *intermediates*, this is an opportunity to check out your game, to locate and eliminate the flaws in technique and tactics alike. Remember when practising to concentrate on your weaknesses, not your strengths; that is the guaranteed way to move up the leagues.

For the *advanced*, this book mirrors the thinking of the professionals. It explains how they play the 'mind game'; how they plan their matches to achieve the right tactical balance; and how they can sometimes turn a losing game into a winning one. It works for them, so it should work for you too.

INTRODUCTION

I was walking away from the Bexley Squash Club with Abou Taleb when he suddenly realized that his pockets were full of practice balls. He turned to look back some 50ft to the shed he used as his pro shop. There was a hole in the roof which he had been planning to mend for the past three weeks. He took his racket and hit each of those balls (a dozen at least) through the hole. They did not even touch the edge.

That was Abou, a magical man who could perform feats on a squash court beyond the dreams of normal men. He would place a ball on the back corner of the service box, play a boast and expect to hit that ball four times out of five. He would stand on the service line, facing the back wall, and volley effortlessly a series of hard-driven shots coming from the front. On his day, he could totally bewilder the very best players in the game.

He was the world champion for three years, and with his gifts, he should have reigned for a decade or more. However, he was too fond of the good life to train the way champions do. So he lost everything he had once held dear: his title,

his family, his friends, and finally his life. Abou died of a heart attack at the age of forty-four.

He has to be the most wasted talent that squash has ever known, but be sure he was not the only one, for this is a game of wasted talent. I doubt very much whether more than five players in every hundred ever achieve anything even close to their full potential.

This is the paradox of squash. Just about every player claims to have a desire to improve, yet only about 5 per cent are prepared to put in the effort which would make this possible.

The reason is that they find practice boring. True, some of the more old-fashioned methods are monotonous, but more modern ideas, notably in condition games, have shown that practice can be very enjoyable indeed, and highly rewarding.

I have always counted myself a lucky man to have been introduced to the game by Abou. He did not just colour my dreams; he widened my horizons, and made me realize that there was a lot more to squash than relentless driving just above the tin.

He taught me the art of deception and no one understood this better than Abou. He encouraged me to master the full range of shots. He made me realize that squash is indeed a form of physical chess, a thinker's game. Above all else, he showed me the pleasure the game can bring.

It is a message that I have endeavoured to pass on to my pupils ever since. This is a game to be enjoyed, and the more you become involved, the greater the pleasure.

Be positive. Don't shackle yourself. I cannot promise to make you all champions because, by definition, there can only be one champion in each category at any given time. However, I can promise to make you a much better player than you are, provided you are prepared to make the necessary effort to listen and to learn.

The listening and the learning must never cease. I have been coaching for twenty years and I am still desperate to learn more. Every week, I play with my friend Hiddy Jahan, the world over-35 champion, and every week I come away a little wiser. For like all the great men of squash down the ages, Hiddy is generous with both his time and his knowledge.

PART I
IN TO PLAY

CHAPTER I

GETTING STARTED

Like so many of the best sports, squash evolved by chance. Boys at Harrow School in the mid-nineteenth century, waiting to take their turn on the rackets courts, had got into the habit of hitting the ball around in an open area with three walls outside the actual court. One day, two of the more imaginative boys turned this into a game, and on that day, squash was born.

The term 'squash' derived from the use of a soft rubber ball which was 'squashed' against the front wall on impact. The sister rebound-sports of fives and rackets use a much harder, non-squashable ball.

In 1883, the first purpose-built court was constructed at Oxford by a Harrow man. It was not until 1911 that the English formalized rules and court dimensions.

For a while, the sport remained largely within the domain of the public schools, gentleman clubs and the services. However, now squash is truly international, a sport of the people, played across the five continents of the world. In Britain alone, there are three million active players.

The attractions are fourfold:

1. It is a very pleasant way to maintain fitness and a sense of well-being.
2. It satisfies a basic desire for competition.
3. It improves one's social life by helping to create an ever-widening circle of friends from both sexes. I don't know many lonely squash players.
4. It is not as time-consuming as sports such as golf or cricket. A 40-minute session on a squash court is guaranteed to wash away the frustrations of a fretful day.

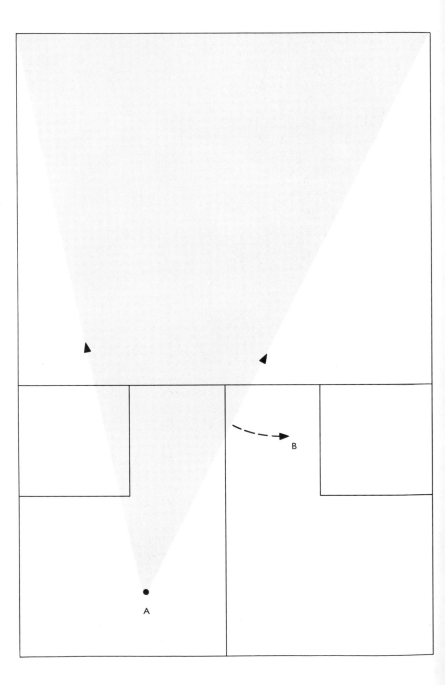

Fig 1   Player A is about to play his shot, and must be given a fair chance of hitting the front wall directly. Therefore, player B must stay out of the shaded area.

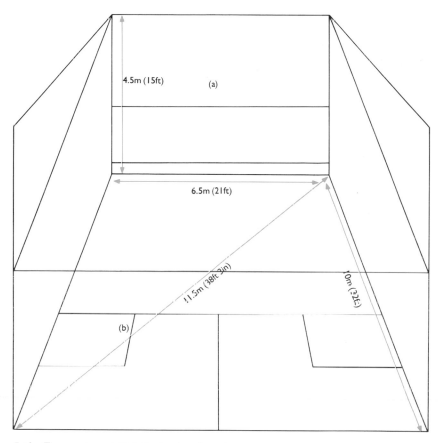

Fig 2   The squash court. Note the two key dimensions: (a) The 5m (15ft) front wall – a target area which provides the opportunity for a wide range of shots; (b) The 15.3m (38ft 3in) diagonal – the tactical path over which to stretch your opponent.

The most basic rule in squash is that the ball must hit and rebound off the front wall above the tin – the lower line, 48cm (19in) above the floor – and stay below the out-of-court line which runs around all four walls.

Hitting is alternate and the striker must play the ball either on the volley or on the first bounce. A rally ends when the receiver does one of three things:

1.   Allows the ball to bounce twice on the floor.
2.   Hits into the tin or above the out-of-court line.
3.   Fails to reach the front wall.

Normally the ball is hit directly on to the front wall, but it may first be hit off any of the walls. This introduces one of the key ideas of squash – angles. The striker must not only anticipate the flight and bounce of a ball, but also consider the angles when executing a shot.

Points are scored in squash only when you are serving. If the receiver wins the rally, he has simply won the right to serve and, therefore, the opportunity to win points.

The server's score is always called first, so a score of 4–6 shows that the server has 4 points and the receiver has 6.

The first player to get 9 points wins the game, unless the score was previously tied at 8–8 (eight all). In that case, the receiver has the choice of whether to play to 9 or 10.

The Basic Rules

Starting the Match

The right to serve first is decided by spinning a racket, i.e. rough or smooth or by some distinguishing mark. If there is no rough or smooth and no distinguishing mark, spin a coin.

Sides

On becoming the server at the start of (or

during) a match, the player decides from which service box (left or right) he wishes to serve. Thereafter, while still winning points, he serves from alternate sides.

A Good Serve

A good serve must go above the cut (service) line and land in the opposite back corner of the court. If it is hit below the cut line or above the out-of-court line, or if the ball fails to drop into the opposite back corner, there is a service change (called a hand-out).

A Foot Fault

The server must have at least one foot completely inside the service box; otherwise this is called a foot fault. Again the service will have been lost. Unlike tennis, you are not given the chance of a second serve.

The rules of squash would be simple if it was not for the fact that two players (four in doubles) share the same territory in a fast and competitive sport. Inevitably, interference occurs and the rules are designed as much for safety as fair play. In the event of interference, a player must stop and ask for a let (a request to have the rally replayed). He is not entitled to a let if he plays or attempts a shot.

The referee will decide whether to award a let, no let or a stroke. In the absence of a referee (i.e. in social and friendly matches) the players will decide by mutual agreement.

No Let

The referee will call 'no let' in any of the following circumstances:

1. If the player would not have got to the ball.
2. If the player did not make sufficient effort to show that he could have got to the ball.
3. If the player attempted the shot and missed. The exception to this is if he hit his opponent on the backswing and appealed immediately. A let is then allowed.

> **KEY POINT**
>
> The close proximity of two competitors who are running, turning and swinging their rackets has its obvious dangers. So always remember that your opponent's safety is in your hands. Learn to swing correctly from the start, and if you feel that either racket or ball may strike your partner, stop and ask for a let.

A Let

The rally is replayed if the player would have got to the ball but for the interference.

A Stroke

The rally is awarded in either of the following circumstances:

1. If the striker was in a winning position.
2. If the striker's opponent had not made enough effort to get out of the way.

Hitting an Opponent with the Ball

If the ball would have hit the front wall first, and been up, had it not been for it hitting the opponent, the striker wins the rally.

If the ball would have hit the side wall first, and then the front, it is a let.

If a player 'turns' in the back corner and hits his opponent, it is a let, provided that the ball would have been up.

Somewhere to Play

Squash centres fall into two categories: public sports (or leisure) centres where courts are hired out to the general public, and private clubs which you have to join before you can play, unless you have a friend who is a member, with whom you can enjoy guest status. There could be a snag here, if your friend sees this simply as an opportunity to dazzle you with his or her array of shots. If this was so, it would be much better to play your initial games

---

with another beginner or with someone prepared to knock the ball around gently and make an effort to help you.

If you wish to take the game up seriously, a local club is your best bet. Then you will soon have a string of playing partners and you will be able to learn a little something from each one. No two players ever have quite the same game.

Before you become too involved, do get some coaching, the earlier the better. Squash is a game of habits, and coaching can help you to develop the right habits.

Clothing

Your local sports shop (or often the club itself) can supply your basic clothing needs: shorts, T-shirts, socks and shoes. The on-court rule used to be strictly all-white. But this has been relaxed and pastel shades (provided they are not too startling) are acceptable at most clubs. However, it would be wise to check *before* you buy.

> **KIT CHECK**
>
> **Shorts and Shirt** Stretch fabrics are ideal. Colours should be white or pastel shades. Shirts with collars and short sleeves are the norm. It is important that they should be comfortable and not restricting.

Take care in your choice of shoes, because in this game they do take a considerable pounding. In addition to being comfortable, they need to be light, strong, supportive and possessed of a good gripping sole. Black soles are prohibited, because they mark the courts.

> **KIT CHECK**
>
> **Shoes** Specialist squash shoes are recommended rather than trainers or old-fashioned plimsolls. They should be light and comfortable with good ankle support. Snug, yet providing plenty of room for the toes. The soles should give good grip and must not be black.

The wearing of two pairs of socks (one thick, one thin) can keep the feet blister-proof, which is a particular peril in the early days before the soles have a chance to become hardened. The legendary Heather McKay wore two pairs right through her long career

Equipment

All you need is a racket and a ball. A lot of clubs hire out rackets or perhaps you can beg, borrow or steal one from a friend who has a bagful. It is often wise to delay buying one of your own until you have some idea of the type that will suit you best.

There are four speeds of ball, each identified by a coloured dot – yellow, white, red and blue in order of increasing speed. For a beginner, the red or blue are good choices. They bounce a little higher and thus give you more time in which to reach them.

Fitness

There is an old adage: 'Don't play squash to get fit. Get fit to play squash'. Be sensible, if you have any doubts about your physical well-being, get your doctor to check you over before you even think of playing. Squash is a physically demanding game, so ease yourself into it gradually.

Court Etiquette

Interference causes more hassle and dents more friendships than anything else in squash. I like to believe that the vast majority of players are basically honest, but inevitably you get some who do not understand the rules, others who suffer from a measure of self-delusion and, let's face it, a few downright cheats.

Make a resolution to be one of the honest ones, to play the game fair from the very start. It is more satisfying that way; you keep your friends and you sleep better too.

Court etiquette is really just another name for good manners. Never walk straight on to a court without first making sure that it is empty. Most doors have a peephole for this purpose. If there are players on the court and their time is up, wait until the end of a rally and then knock. If they do not respond (or hear), knock again.

At the end of your game, shake hands, say something pleasant and do remember to thank the marker. If you have lost, smile through the pain. If you have won, invite your opponent to have a drink – strong, soft, coffee, tea or whatever. It is a friendly custom and one that helps to make squash such an attractive social game.

A word of warning: squash is an addiction and you may well become hooked for life.

Terminology

Squash has inherited its own language and it is useful to understand the various terms from the start.

Boast A shot played into the near-side wall so that it rebounds on to the front wall. This is also known as an 'angle'.

Clinger A shot that runs so close to the wall that it appears literally to cling.

Cut Backspin applied to the ball so that it will 'sit down' quickly.

Die or dying This is when the second bounce of a shot stops dead on or near the side or back walls. A ball can also die by being hit directly into the nick. This is called a dead nick.

Drop shot A soft shot played to drop into the front corners.

Hand-out The player who receives the

service. Also the expression used to indicate a service change.

Kill   A heavily cut, hard, low drive.

Knock-up   A period of five minutes, before the match starts, during which players practise by hitting across to one another.

Length   A straight or crosscourt shot designed to force your opponent into the back corners.

Loose   A weak shot that comes out too far from the side wall.

Lob   A soft shot designed to go over your opponent and drop in the back corner.

Nick   The junction of the walls and floor.

Reverse angle   A boast played on to the far-side wall, as distinct from the near-side wall.

Turning   This normally occurs when the ball strikes the back wall at an angle, and the receiver beaten, say, on the backhand, turns through 180 degrees and plays it on the forehand, or vice versa.

Width   A shot angled wide across court and designed to beat the opponent's volley.

Fig 3   The T can get a little crowded. Jansher Khan and a headless Chris Dittmar.

KIT CHECK

Sports Bag   Plastic is more practical than leather, as it will contain wet kit and wet towels from time to time. In addition to your squash kit and racket, the contents should include: two towels (a small one to take on court and a larger one for showering); a spare racket; a spare shirt (for a possible quick change between games); a spare ball; a spare grip; foot powder; resin (for the racket handle); and a small first-aid kit.

Summary

1.   Do check the club rules on guest fees, placing bags, clothes on court, etc.
2.   Don't buy an expensive racket until you have had the chance to discover which type suits you best, as regards weight, balance, width of handle, etc.
3.   Do select your first playing partner with care.
4.   Don't wear black-soled shoes on court.
5.   Do get some early coaching.
6.   Don't open a court door while a rally is in progress – it is dangerous.
7.   Do knock on the court door and wait when it is your time to play.
8.   Don't go to the bar in wet kit, unless there is a sweat bar.
9.   Do be pleasant and enjoy the game's social side.
10.   Don't arrive late for a game, because with courts often heavily booked, it may become a very brief game.

CHAPTER 2

THE FIRM FOUNDATION

When the former world champion, Geoff Hunt, first learnt squash, he did not play a single game for three months, because his father wanted to be sure that he had first of all mastered the basics of the game.

As a coach, I can appreciate the wisdom of that move. I have spent much of my teaching life correcting the faults that my pupils developed in those early days, simply because there had been no one to guide them in this the most impressionable stage. Bad habits are easy to acquire, but desperately hard to lose.

I am not suggesting that you follow Geoff Hunt's example to the letter and wait three months before playing your first game. Geoff's ambitions were more far-reaching than those of most mortals. Even at that age, he was determined to be the best.

However, the central message is clear: make sure you master the basics before you become too involved in match play. Then everything else will follow smoothly.

In essence, this means:

1. Gaining control over both racket and ball.
2. Moving and positioning correctly.

The Grip

The normal grip used in squash is known as the 'continental' or 'shake-hands grip'. As this is the most basic of all squash habits, I cannot overstress the importance of getting it right from the start. Let's take it in stages:

1. Using the left hand, assuming that you are right-handed, dangle the racket by the neck. If you are holding it correctly, you will not be able to see the strings, just the frame.

Figs 4 (a) and (b)   The grip.

(a)   Hold the neck of the racket with the left hand.

(b)   Shake hands with the right. This is why it is sometimes known as the 'shake hands grip'.

2. Shake hands with the handle of the racket. Spread the fingers of the gripping hand, so that a 'V' is formed between the thumb and forefinger. This V should point along the left hand shaft of the racket.
3. The heel of your hand should be about 2–3cm (1in), from the butt with your index finger curled around the handle, like the trigger of a gun.
4. The three remaining fingers are curled around the handle, with the thumb resting on the second finger.

This is the conventional grip used by just about every squash-playing nation. However, I often encourage my more ambitious pupils to adopt what I term the

'Jahangir grip'. To demonstrate this, I ask them to hold the racket in the normal way and then I twist it an eighth of the way round in a clockwise direction to open up the face. The racket turns, but the hand remains in the same position.

The reason I restrict this to the more ambitious is that it feels odd at first, and

---

KIT CHECK

Grips   Towelling grips are the most popular. In addition to improving your holding power, they will help to mould the handle to the size that suits you best.

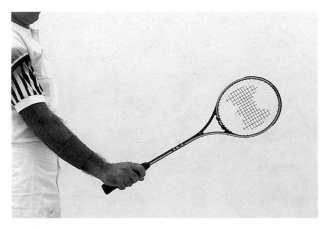

Fig 5 (a)   The grip viewed from the back of the hand. Note the position of the forefinger (the trigger finger).

(b)   The grip viewed from the front of the hand. Note the 'V' formed between forefinger and thumb.

Fig 6 (a)   The classic side-on stance (forehand). On both forehand and backhand, you lead into the shot on your front foot. The knees are bent, the body balanced and the wrist cocked.

Fig 6 (b)   The classic side-on stance (backhand).

consequently frustrating. Racket handles are not designed to be held that way. However, with patience and perseverance, it will soon begin to feel quite natural.

There are several advantages: the more open face will automatically impart cut to the ball, making it sit down quicker; you are less likely to hit tin, and it also gives greater control on the volleys. Jahangir and many of the world's top players now use this grip and, incidentally, so do I.

Remember, feel and touch are supplied by your fingers, so it is important that they, rather than the palm of your hand, supply the pressure. The grip is the same for both forehand and backhand. In squash, unlike tennis, there just is not time to change it during the course of a rally.

Ball Control

This is simply the ability to make the ball connect with the centre of the racket. If you have not played a racket sport before, it may seem a little strange at first, but don't despair. Practice will soon solve the problem. Initially, you will not even need to step on to the court. Hold your racket at arm's length with the face horizontal, and see how many times you can bounce the ball on it continuously. Begin with 10 as your target then progress to 100. Then bounce the ball on alternate sides of the racket, again beginning with a target of 10 and advancing to a 100.

For the next stage, go on to court, stand 2m (6½ft) from the front wall and pat the ball underarm against the wall. Then retreat slowly down the court, hitting the ball steadily higher on the front wall to get

the extra depth. Once you have reached the back wall, retrace your steps. Only this time, you will need to hit the ball progressively lower on the front wall as you advance up the court.

The Racket

It is important to understand from an early stage that the angle of the racket face at the moment of impact determines the path that the ball will follow:

1. If the racket face was 45 degrees open, the ball would travel on a diagonal course, bisecting the right angle.
2. If the face was totally closed (in other words, forming a right angle with the floor), the ball would travel parallel to the floor.
3. If the face was parallel to the front wall, the ball would travel parallel to the side wall.

Generally, in squash you use an open face. This is used to hit upwards on the ball, to

provide cut, to provide feel on some shots and to help take the pace off the ball. The more you open the racket face, the more strings you have to meet the ball at the striking point.

The Cocked Wrist

You should always keep the racket head raised above the level of your wrist, so that the handle forms an angle of approximately 90 degrees with the forearm. This is a cocked wrist and it should remain cocked from the start of the backswing and throughout the whole shot.

There is a belief that squash needs a 'wristy' action. This is misleading. If you simply concentrate upon keeping your wrist firm, everything will just happen naturally. If the grip is correct, a cocked wrist will tighten of its own accord.

Hiddy Jahan has the best wrist in squash. He is a big man with tremendous power who hits the ball harder than anyone in the world. I remember him once bursting three balls in a single game. His wrist was first developed during his early days as a

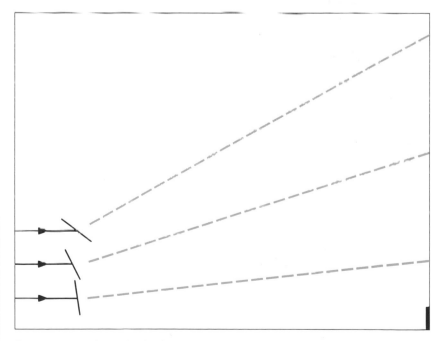

Fig 7   The angle of the racket face (whether open or closed) determines the angle of flight.

top badminton player in Pakistan. His power comes from the transference of weight and that very good wrist.

He often uses a surprisingly short backswing, and so is able to keep the same sort of swing for a soft drop, a drive to length and the cannonball kill. These are key elements of deception. The Australian, Ricki Hill, is one of many players who find it almost impossible to read Hiddy. He would be the first to admit that a large part of the secret behind that awesome power is the timing.

Occasionally, when you are short of space, you need to drop or break your wrist. But always try to keep such moments to a minimum, because they lead to less control in both shots and technique.

The Swing

The swing can be likened to the action of skimming a flat stone across water, or that of a cricketer throwing the ball flat to the wicket keeper. Take your arm back as though you were going to do just that, only instead of a stone or a ball, you have a racket in your hand – and you will not (hopefully) let go.

Now if the wrist is cocked, the racket head will automatically have been raised to a position close to the right ear for the forehand (left ear for the backhand). The arm is bent at the elbow and a comfortable distance away from the body.

The downswing creates the racket-head speed. The faster the downswing, the harder the ball will be hit. From the top of the backswing, the racket will begin its descent almost vertically, and then travel through a curve so that at the moment of impact, it will be travelling parallel to the floor.

Two important tips are:

1.   Keep the head of the racket above the wrist throughout the swing; otherwise, you will lose both power and control.
2.   After impact, make sure that the racket head follows through for at least another 30cm (1ft) in the same direction. This is one of the reasons why many players lose power on the drive. Their racket rises too soon from the horizontal.

Vary the size of your swing according to the shot: a fuller swing for power; a shorter swing for touch. Do not allow it to become too much of a flourish. A compact swing is far less prone to error and can be produced so much more quickly in a game where time can be in short supply. Remember the overall aim is to produce a smooth, flowing, grooved swing which will become totally automatic.

The safety of your opponent is another important factor. The swing should begin in the vicinity of one ear and finish beside the other (both your own). If you follow through for that extra 30cm (1ft) as I have suggested, you will find that your arm bends automatically, raising your racket above head height.

The swing is one of the great oddities of squash. To a golfer of almost any standard, the swing is a religion. He will consequently seek advice about it from his pro; he will watch television avidly as the swings of top players are dissected by the commentators, and more than likely he will be seen knocking divots out of his lawn on a Sunday morning in a bid to achieve the perfect swing.

The swing is every bit as important to the squash player. It is, after all, the basis from which everything else springs. If you cannot hit the ball correctly, how can you ever hope to make any real progress? Yet only a handful of players in any club ever make any real effort to get it right.

The Racket Axis

The axis of the racket is an imaginary line drawn from the butt to the lower edge of the frame at the moment of impact. Ideally this line should be parallel to the floor; if the face is also open, it becomes virtually impossible to hit tin. Obviously this cannot apply to overheads or high volleys, but for any shot played between knee or waist height, it becomes a very good guide to follow.

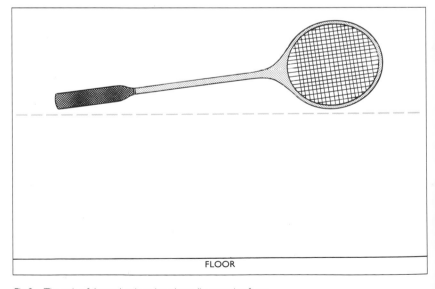

FLOOR

Fig 8   The axis of the racket is an imaginary line running from the butt to the lower edge of the racket head. Keep the axis parallel to the floor and the racket face open; it then becomes virtually impossible to hit tin.

The Knees

In squash, you need to bend your knees much more than you do in other racket sports, because after bouncing, the ball stays so close to the floor.

A reluctance to do so is the basic cause of many errors, so make sure you build the habit into your game. Then you will find that you have gained three advantages:

1. The relationship between your racket and forearm will be correct on impact.
2. Your eyes will be looking along the line of flight as the ball comes to you.
3. You will be able to regain the T much more rapidly from a bent-knee position – rather like a sprinter coming out of his blocks.

Positioning

One of the main problems in squash is that players run to the ball. Don't do this; move to the place from which you want to hit it. This is positioning.

> **STAR TIP**
>
> *If you wish to move well, first learn to chassis.*
>
> Jahangir Khan

The beginner's tendency to run straight at the ball is a very natural one, but the inevitable result is a cramped position (much too close to the ball) and, therefore, with no chance of playing a smooth shot.

As the squash hitting action is side-arm, we need to position side-on to the direction we want to hit the ball. This very simple idea of being in the right place for your shot is one of the most important in squash.

Court Movement

You may have complete command of all the shots, perfect co-ordination and the tactical wisdom of a Solomon, but unless

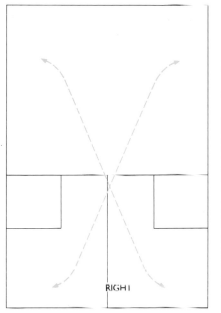
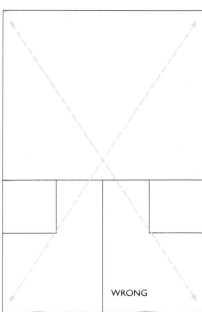

Fig 9 Don't run to the ball. Run to the place from which you wish to hit the ball.

you can actually reach the ball with time to spare, these qualities will be of little use. Therefore, it is perhaps not surprising that all the top players, without exception, move well. Jansher just seems to glide, Zarak is lightning fast and Jahangir has the steps of a dancer. Make movement your priority too. For without it, any progress you wish to make has to be limited.

This does not mean that you need to be an athlete or a gymnast to succeed. It simply means that you have to learn to shrink the court by moving early and following the right path to the ball. Ideally, all movement should begin from the T or, more precisely, from the area surrounding the junction of the short line and the half-court line.

Let's consider movement from the T to the front corners of the court. Do not run diagonally otherwise you will be committing the cardinal sin of running straight at the ball. You will arrive half-facing the front wall, cramped for room, and probably wind up playing a loose crosscourt.

Your initial movement should be straight towards the front wall followed by a

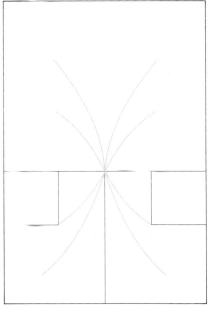

Fig 10 Court movement pattern, showing the paths which you follow from the T to the ball, and back again.

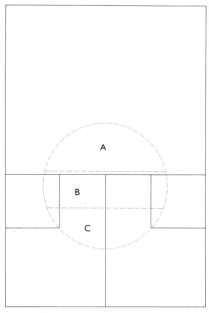

Fig 11   The T-area. Always look upon the T as an area, rather than a definite spot upon the court, and then learn to read the game and position accordingly. In area A, if you have good reason to believe your opponent is about to play short. In area B, if you are uncertain about his intentions. In area C, if you have good reason to believe he is about to play deep.

sideways step towards the ball with either the left or right foot, according to whether you are playing a forehand or backhand. You thus arrive facing the side wall and in position to play your shot.

The path you take is L-shaped with a curve softening the angle. You follow the same L-shaped path to the back corners of the court – down the middle and then across towards the ball.

The return route is equally important for two reasons:

1.   To ensure that you do not impede your opponent.
2.   To regain the T position as swiftly and smoothly as possible.

The initial movement from a corner should be towards the opposite side wall, then back to the T, keeping your eye on the ball at all times. In other words, it is a reversal of the L-shaped path that took you to the corner in the first place.

Good squash movement is not the same thing as running fast. It involves many different steps. There are jumps, hops,

---

KEY POINT

After playing a shot in the forecourt, never turn your back on either the front wall or your opponent, as you move back towards the T. Use sideways movement so that you can follow the flight of the ball during its two-way journey: on to your opponent's racket and back again.

---

lunges, slides and chassis movements. Hashim, one of the fastest ever players around a court, was a great believer in a big first step. Others prefer a big last step, which is fine, just so long as you finish up in a balanced position. The method you choose to move over that L-shaped path is an individual one. Experiment and discover the way that suits you best.

Good movement really can help to cut a court down to size. As the walls restrict your swing, it makes good sense to stay well clear of them. Picture a corridor, the width of the service box, running parallel to each side wall. Regard this as a no-go area and, at most, place only one foot in it to play your shot.

I know that on one's bad days, the court can appear too large for comfort as we are forced to scramble but, in reality, we are operating in a very small area. The furthest distance from the T (that to the front corners) is only three full strides away. A lot of down-the-wall shots can be reached with a single stride.

STAR TIP

There isn't a player at any level who doesn't feel less exposed if he lays back a bit behind the T.

Jonah Barrington

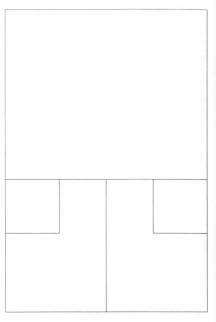

Fig 12   The no-go areas. When playing your standard shots, put only one foot at most into the shaded areas. This is part of the secret of cutting the court down to size.

During the course of a rally, you stop just twice: when on the T and when about to play your shot. Because of the nature of the game, both stoppages are liable to be brief, but nevertheless the positions adopted at these times will be crucial.

Your position on the T will depend upon the whereabouts of your opponent:

1.   If your opponent is in front of you, place your feet on either side of the half-court line with your toes pointing towards the front wall. Crouch with knees bent. Stay on your toes or the balls of your feet, never on your heels. Keep your racket up. You are now in good shape to cover both the forehand and backhand. Turn your head and shoulders to watch your opponent and the ball.
2.   If your opponent is alongside or behind you, position your feet and body so that you are at an angle of 45 degrees to the side wall. This makes it so much easier for you to watch him play his stroke and to follow the path of the ball both before and

Fig 13   Hiddy Jahan at full stretch, driving the ball deep down the forehand wall. When time is short, the feet must improvize.

after it is struck. On the backhand side of the court, your left foot will be nearest to the back wall; while on the forehand side, the right foot will be nearest. When taking up this angled position, be prepared for a shot hit across court and targeted into the corner behind you, because you will need to turn through 90 degrees to reach it. Provided you are watching as his racket head hits through the ball, this should not really pose a problem.

As always, be flexible. Do not take up a static position simply because you have read about it in a coaching manual (even mine), if you have a good reason for not doing so.

For instance, your opponent may be standing just in front of you and you will be too close to his backswing for comfort, or maybe he is a little further forward, but blocking your view of the ball he is about to play. In that case, move to the side so

Fig 14   The three classic positions for the feet:
(a) The open stance, for all crosscourts;
(b) The basic stance, for all straight shots;
(c) The back corner stance, for back-corner boasts.

that you will be able to see both racket and ball at the moment of impact. You will also be creating a clearer path for yourself as you move towards your next shot.

Feet hold the key to the three main striking positions. For the sake of simplicity, these three positions are for the forehand.

The Basic Stance
This is for such shots as the straight drive, straight lob, straight drop and trickle boast:

1.   Face the right-hand wall and point the left toe directly towards the wall, creating an angle of 90 degrees.

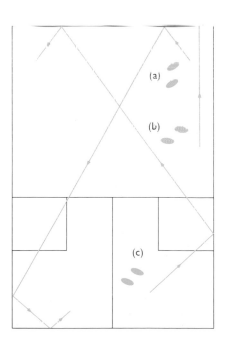

2. Keep your feet just over a shoulder's width apart in a comfortable, balanced position.

3. Place the right foot about 30cm (1ft) further away from the wall than the left, with the toe pointing slightly backwards.

The Open Stance

This is for such shots as the crosscourt drive, the crosscourt lob, the crosscourt drop and reverse angle.

1. Point the left toe directly into the front right hand corner of the court.

2. Your right toe will be nearer the side wall and pointing directly at it.

The Back-Corner Stance

This is for the back-court boast.

1. Point your feet to either side of the back right-hand corner.

2. Bend the knees so that they obscure the view of your toes.

The Wrong Foot

These are the three classic positions and the ones you should try to adopt, but we have to realize that in a game which can be as fast and as furious as squash, it will not always be possible to adopt the correct stance, so quite often we will be forced to hit off the wrong foot. When this happens, the natural tendency is to hit the ball crosscourt, quite regardless of whether or not this was the right shot to play.

It is important to learn how to send the ball in the desired direction, even when the feet are wrong. Jahangir has a practice routine in which he hits alternate drives off the right and wrong feet. This is a good tip for us all to follow.

There is also a strong case for suggesting that 'wrong' is very often 'right' when you are playing a shot on the forehand, particularly behind the short line.

Geoff Hunt was one of the first major players consistently to play off his 'wrong' foot in that area. He did this partly because it made it easier for him to regain the T swiftly and cover his own shot. He did not need to turn through 180 degrees, but could instead push off with the right foot

and be back in position within a couple of strides.

He also felt that the conventional back-corner stance (or squat stance, as it is sometimes called) was too restricting on his choice of shot. Of course, he was quite right. It limits you to the boast, and that is not the shot most of us would choose to play in that situation. An experienced opponent, having seen the squat stance, will have anticipated the boast and be already planning the quick drop riposte. This means that you will need to move over the full length of the diagonal to reach the ball and probably be forced to scramble.

Therefore, whenever possible, 'straighten' the ball out from those back-corner positions on the forehand side. This really does mean turning yourself around and playing off the 'wrong' foot.

Your aim, then, should be to hit well above the cut line, and bring the ball high and tight down the side wall, thus putting your opponent back into the corner from which you have just emerged.

The reason why these problems are confined to the forehand is that the body is in the way and once turned will block the line of your own shot. On the backhand, the arm flows free and there are no restraints.

Contact

When playing our shots, we do not enjoy the luxuries of a golfer who has all the time in the world to place his feet beside a stationary ball, but we must nevertheless be thinking along somewhat similar lines. It helps to have a mental picture of ourselves in that brief moment before contact.

Let's assume we are playing a forehand drive down the wall. Our feet are in the right place, our weight is being transferred on to the left leg, and we are just about to make contact in front of the leading foot. The racket face is parallel to the front wall and will remain so during the follow through. That is the image you need to store in the back of your mind. Conjure it up constantly and the shot will eventually become automatic.

Geometry

Squash is a rebound sport, so you need to learn the geometry of the court, i.e. the angle and elevation with which to send a ball to the front wall *en route* to its chosen destination or, much more complicated, the angle for a three-wall boast designed to die in the nick.

You will learn much of this from trial and error, but here are a few guide-lines on placement:

1. Use the top part of the front wall for your defensive game.

2. Use the middle part for your pressure game.

3. Use the bottom part for your attacking game.

4. Remember to leave a margin for error.

5. To get good length, hit above the cut line.

6. From the back court, lift drives above the cut line.

7. When crosscourting from the back, aim at the far half of the front wall.

8. Target the four corners.

9. Concentrate on good length and width.

10. Do not forget the third dimension: height.

Ghosting

This is a way of improving your court movement, made famous by Jonah Barrington. You simply play an imaginary game against an imaginary opponent. You have a racket, but no ball. You move, say, from the T to the front right-hand corner, play a shadow shot, then recover to the T, and so on.

If you are going to get the true value out of this exercise, three things are vital:

KEY POINT

Never hit a shot that finishes in the middle of the court. To a good opponent, this is just cannon-fodder.

Fig 15   Chris Walker in play against Fredrik Johnson. Final strides such as this can cut the court down to size

1.   You must move correctly, concentrating on good footwork.
2.   You must play a correct stroke.
3.   You must get back to the T between shots and watch the imaginary ball. In other words, play it for real.

Summary

Stroke Making

1.   Use the same grip for forehand and backhand.
2.   Keep the wrist cocked.
3.   At impact, imagine you are skimming a flat stone across the water.
4.   After impact, make sure that the racket head follows through for at least 30cm (1ft) in the same direction.
5.   Keep the racket face open.
6.   Watch the ball right on to your racket.
7.   Swing from a V to a V.
8.   When swinging, keep the shoulders still.
9.   Strike the ball (on the forehand) as it crosses the line of your leading foot.
10.   Strike the ball (on the backhand) 30cm (1ft) before it crosses the line of your leading foot.

Movement and Positioning

1.   Do not run to the ball; run to the place from which you want to hit it.
2.   Stop only twice in a rally: when on the T and when about to play your shot.
3.   After playing your shot, return to the T as swiftly as possible.
4.   In the T area, stay on your toes and the balls of your feet, never on your heels.
5.   Achieve early movement by watching your opponent.
6.   Cut the court down to size by staying out of the no-go areas (marked on Fig 11).
7.   Practise playing off the 'wrong' foot, as well as the 'correct' foot.
8.   From the T, follow an L shaped path towards the four corners.
9.   When returning to the T, retrace your steps along that selfsame L-shaped path.
10.   Improve your court movement by ghosting.

CHAPTER 3

THE SERVICE

Too many squash players tend to look upon the serve as simply a means of starting a rally, but it is more than that, although admittedly, it can never have the value it has in tennis, where champions such as John McEnroe and Boris Becker base their entire game upon a powerful, heavily cut serve.

Their squash counterparts, Jahangir and Jansher, may appear casual by comparison, but this is usually misleading. Squash professionals are not aiming to hit a pure tennis-type ace direct from a serve, but they are nevertheless seeking to get an advantage by putting their opponent on the defensive and thus gaining an early command of the rally which follows.

Mopped Up!

I was playing my first-ever game with Azam Khan at the Grampians Club in West London. I was about to serve when I realized he was mopping his brow. The handkerchief was in his right hand, the racket in his left. I paused and waited. 'No, no, Eric,' he said, 'go ahead'. I hit what I considered to be a pretty good serve. Azam nonchalantly killed it stone dead in the nick. He then put his handkerchief away and transferred the racket to his normal hand. The right.

It is different at the other end of the spectrum. A beginner who acquires, for instance, a reasonable lob serve may gain a considerable advantage over his opponents, provided that they are beginners too. They will find difficulty in playing volleys close to the wall and they will not enjoy the challenge of hitting the ball out of the back corners.

This is one of the most valuable early lessons you can learn in squash. If a situation troubles you, the chances are that it will trouble your opponent too. So let this influence your choice of shots.

As you improve and begin to move up the leagues, you will find that points won directly from the serve become an ever-increasing rarity. Therefore there is a tendency to place less importance upon the serve. This is a big mistake. Even amongst top players, a good serve is still worth about three points a game. Only at this level you will be seeking to force weak returns rather than hit service aces.

I remember once listening to a man who regularly went down the Cresta Run, that icy chute which sweeps down the mountain at St. Moritz. He said that when you make a bad mistake on one of the bends, you know you are bound to crash, but the really frightening thing about this is that you will not crash immediately. You will have time to think. Each succeeding bend will multiply that original mistake and you will probably fly off about five bends later. It is a bit like that sometimes when you make a mistake in a rally. A good opponent will not give you the chance to recover, and with each succeeding shot,

your position will become steadily more desperate.

It is a fact that the player who takes the initial command in a rally usually wins it. This is why those opening two shots, the service and return, are so important.

When serving, you have been given a rare opportunity to take command of the rally to follow. You are not being moved or rushed. The ball is in your hand. You can take your time. You are in the driving seat, so keep it that way.

KEY POINT

Whichever type of serve you use, be careful with the throw-up. This is almost as important in squash, as it is in tennis. If you wish to develop a consistent serve, a consistent throw-up is imperative.

When receiving a serve, get your early warning system going by watching the server. As soon as the ball is on the way, draw the racket back so that you can swing smoothly into the stroke; and if you need to move your feet, do so early.

Your initial objectives have to be:

1. To make sure the ball hits the side wall before your opponent plays it.
2. To limit his options to a back-corner boast.

Figs 16 (a)–(f)   The Service

Fig 16 (a)   When serving, take up position as near the centre as possible to minimize the angle.

(b)   The semi-lob serve (from the right). Contact is made well in front of the body with an open racket face

(c)   The flat serve (from the right). The ball is being aimed approximately 1m (3ft) above the cut line.

(d)   The flat serve (from the left). You can achieve a much tighter angle from this side.

(e)   As you follow through, allow your own momentum to make that first step towards the T.

(f)   Hiddy is poised on the T with his head turned to follow the flight of the ball.

The cardinal sins to avoid are:

1. Serving out.
2. Giving your opponent a free volley.
3. Leaving it short.
4. Over hitting so that the ball comes easily off the back wall.
5. Striking the side wall so hard and at such an angle that the ball rebounds towards centre court.

The serve can be looked upon as a mechanical shot, and consistency must be achieved. You can place your feet in the same place every time, aim at the same part of the front wall, use the same swing and the same degree of force. If there is a mark on the wall somewhere near your target, use this as an aiming guide. Like a naval gunner, be prepared to readjust your sights.

Rules

1. To be good, the serve must first strike the front wall above the cut line and land in the opposite back corner of the court.

2. The server must have at least one foot clearly inside the service box, not touching any of the lines.
3. If the ball is served 'out' or a foot fault occurs, there is a service change (called a hand-out). The days of second serves are long gone.

The Serves

It is important to have a basic serve that is both secure and effective. The most commonly used is the semi-lob service, because it meets both these requirements. But before we describe this in detail, bear one thing in mind.

The server starts with a pyschological and tactical advantage over the non-server. The server can win points, cannot lose them and can therefore afford to be more aggressive.

I advise my pupils to have two main basic serves, intermingled with a host of variations. Those two basic serves are usually the semi-lob from the right-hand box and the hard, flat serve from the left-hand box.

The Semi-Lob Serve

The semi-lob is not so devastating as a well played full-lob serve, but it is a lot safer, and so is much more of a percentage shot. It is less likely to hit above the out-of-court line and yet can still pose problems to the receiver. As when using all serves, set out to narrow the angle by standing as near to the centre line as possible. Because good width is so important, you want the ball to stay as tight as possible to the side wall and hopefully even tighter to the back wall.

Look upon the serve as a crosscourt. This means that you adopt the open stance. When serving from the right-hand box, you face the right-hand front corner. Your left foot will be positioned close to the short line, and pointing directly into that right-hand corner.

Serve underarm with an open racket and aim about 90cm (3ft) below the top line and maybe 60cm (2ft) to the left of centre on the front wall.

Your object is to make gentle contact (just a kiss) high on the side wall near the back of the service box. The ball should

Fig 17   The flight path of the ball for the semi-lob serve from the right-hand box.

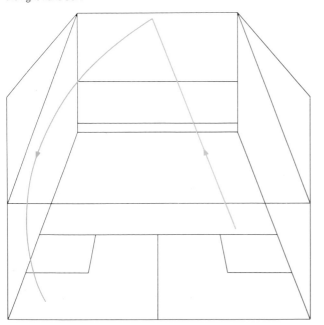

Fig 18   The flight path for the semi-lob serve from the left-hand box.

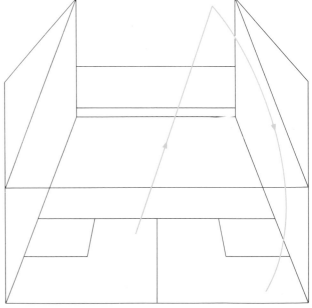

then hit the floor and back wall (in that order), finishing up tight in the corner.

As soon as you have served, move on to the T. Allow the momentum of your swing to take you automatically in that direction. But remember that we do not have any God-given right to the T position. We can only be there when we are not in any danger of impeding our opponent's shot. So if, for instance, our serve has struck the side wall too hard and at too great an angle, sending the ball bouncing out into centre court, we must stay away from the T for three very good reasons:

1. If the receiver plays a shot from that position, we will be in the direct line of fire.
2. If the ball strikes us, we will automatically lose the point – assuming that the ball would have carried directly to the front wall – and that is a doubly painful way to lose a point.
3. If the receiver stepped away from the ball and appealed to the marker, you could well have a stroke awarded against you.

We will assume our serve has stayed close to the side wall and we have a right to the T. Do not forget to turn your head to watch the flight of the ball right on to your opponent's racket. A surprising number of players serve and then become front wall watchers. By so doing, they surrender their advantage.

The Hard, Flat Serve

Look upon this as a forehand volley hit at shoulder height. From the left-hand service box, face the right-hand wall in the normal basic stance, and strike the ball as close to the half-court line as possible. The angle will be narrower this time; you will be aiming about (90cm) 3ft to the right of centre on the front wall, and approximately (60cm) 2ft above the cut line. Your target will again be centred around the back of the service box, but you will be striking the side wall much lower. Otherwise, with the extra pace on the ball, it would be bouncing much too freely off the back wall.

Many receivers virtually face the side wall, believing that your serve will never change.

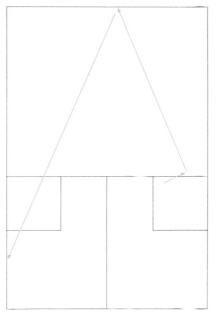

Fig 19   The flight path for the flat serve from the right.

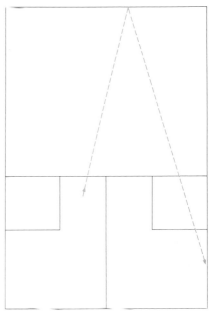

Fig 20   The flight path for the flat serve from the left.

This is the time to place doubt in their minds. Fire your next serve straight at their body (ideally at the shoulder). Alternatively, put it just behind them, targeted for the corner. As a surprise serve, this can be very effective.

In a bid to break up your serving rhythm, some players will take a step closer to the wall with the intention of attacking the serve as it crosses the short line. Again make the back corner your target. Remember the deeper the position adopted by the receiver, the deeper you can target the serve.

The high backhand volley is probably the most fragile of all shots. Players will mishit a couple and suddenly lose their confidence. Then they start looking for options. Take advantage of this common chink. Play your lobs high enough to discourage the early attacking volley, and let them just kiss the wall so that they stay tight. Make width your ally.

Variations

Although the semi-lob and the hard flat serves are recommended for basic use, it is important to learn others too, so that you can introduce the element of surprise. By ringing the changes, you can often unsettle an opponent who has been handling your service with some confidence.

If you ever get the opportunity to watch Jahangir, you will see him vary his serves from a lob to a smash and also throw in the odd 'bouncer' when going for the back-wall nick.

The Full Lob

This is a very effective serve, but risky with a small margin for error. The ball is hit high on the front wall and designed to arc up close to the lights, strike the side wall just under the out-of-court line and then fall almost dead in the corner. If to be used in a match, it will need a lot of practice beforehand. Otherwise stick to the semi-lob.

The Cling Lob

This is a high service aimed to go over the receiver's head, rebound off the back and move into the side wall to cling or at least restrict the return of a straight shot.

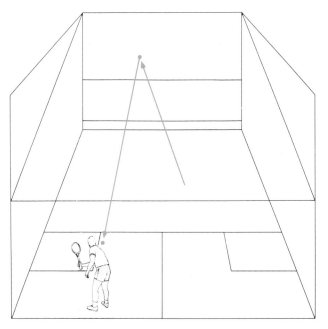

Fig 21   The flight path for the bodyline serve.

Fig 22   The flight path for the corkscrew serve.

The Smash

This is a hard service, using the overarm tennis action. It is often aimed at the side-wall nick behind the service box and, occasionally, the back-wall nick.

The Backhand

This can be done from the right service box only. It provides a good view of the receiver and easy access to the T. It also narrows down the angle, which is an aid to width.

The Bodyline

As the name suggests, this is a hard service aimed straight at the body, ideally at the shoulder. It is very much a surprise shot, which is intended to catch the receiver flat-footed.

The Corkscrew

This is another surprise shot and only to be used very rarely. The ball is hit high on to the front wall and as near the corner (on the server's side) as possible, so that, having struck both walls, it will screw out and travel diagonally until it hits the opposite side wall. Here the spin imparted

from the front corner will cause the ball to rebound at a right angle and parallel to the back wall.

Check-List

As an aid to concentration, it is helpful to have your own check-list when about to serve:

1. Check the position of your feet.
2. Check your front-wall target spot.
3. Check the position of the receiver.

Receiving a Serve

When receiving, your first objective has to be that of reversing the roles – putting the server into the back corner and yourself on the T. Your overall targets will be the four corners of the court but, in reality, 80 per cent of your shots will be directed back down the wall. The comforting thought has to be that you know the serve has to fall into this set area of the court, which is less than a quarter of the total floor space. Therefore, provided you can

volley, the actual task of getting it back should not pose any problems. It is really the question of how deep and how tight you can keep your length and width that will determine your success.

Stance

It is best to adopt an open-chested stance to avoid the danger of being surprised by the bodyline serve or one aimed behind you for the corner. When receiving, stay alert and use your feet. Possibly because this is a static situation, a surprising number of players get caught flat-footed when the unexpected shots arrive.

Do watch the server and follow the ball in flight. Unless it is a hot court or the server is hitting too hard, try to prevent the ball reaching the back wall. Only boast when you want to – not when your opponent wants you to.

Turning

Make a resolution never to turn, partly because it is dangerous, and partly because it is bad tactics. If the ball is bouncing wide

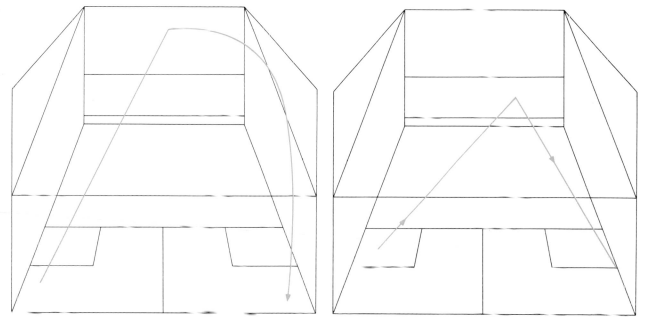

Fig 23   A return of serve – the lob.

Fig 24   A return of serve – the crosscourt drive or volley.

Fig 25   A return of serve – the straight drive or volley.

Fig 26   A return of serve – a straight drop or crosscourt drop.

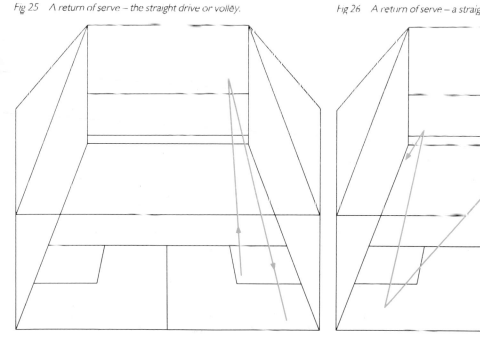

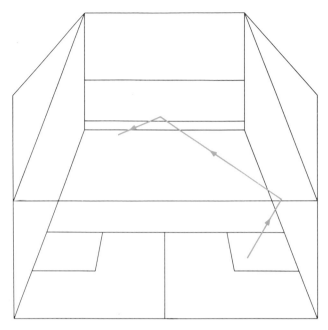

Fig 27   A return of serve – the boast.

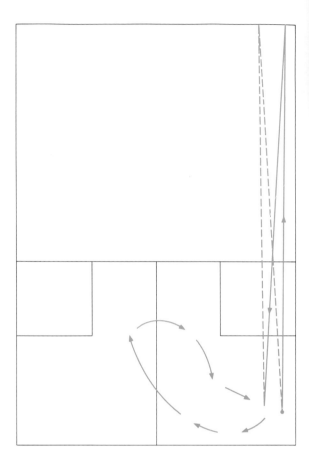

Fig 28   The correct circling movement from the T to the back corner, returning to the T via the half-court line. Note: from the right, you circle clockwise, and from the left, anti-clockwise.

off the side wall, back towards the half-court line or beyond, play it on the backhand, assuming, of course, that you are in the left-hand court.

By so doing, you will have forced the server out of position. He will not be able to get to the T, because he would be blocking your shot, and he will not be able to cross your line of fire. Therefore, he will be starting late and quite possibly having to cover two-thirds of the court.

The Receiver's Options

These are the options in order of preference:

1.   Volley before the ball hits the side.
2.   Volley after it hits the side.
3.   Drive before the ball hits the back.
4.   Drive after it hits the back.
5.   Boast.

Variations

Most of the variations for the return of serve come with the volley from the front of the box. Generally, it is wiser to play straight. The straight volley to dying length, the volley kill and the volley drop are comparatively safe returns which can put the server under pressure.

After a series of shots down the wall, the server may start to crowd you. This is the time for a crosscourt drive, which is hit hard and targeted for the back of the service box. If played well, it will probably wrong-foot the server. Equally importantly, it will put doubts in his mind and encourage him to stay in centre court. Alternatively, a high crosscourt lob can pay unexpected dividends, if used sparingly.

When receiving do not become too predictable. If you hit every return up the side wall, your opponent will be able to move further and further over from the T, looking for an interception. If in trouble, be positive. Do something about it. Change position, so that he has to switch his own

---

STAR TIP

Make the wall your friend.

Azam Khan

Figs 29 (a)–(d)   Circling.

Figs 29 (a)–(d)   This is a vital technique to master, in order that you don't impede your opponent, and that you regain the T as smoothly as possible.

(a)

(b)

(c)

(d)

Figs 30 (a)–(h)   The return of serve.

Figs 30 (a)–(h)   (a)   The position of the receiver. Remain comfortably balanced and watch the server, so that you have ample time to move if the need arises. The receiving options in order of preference: (b)   Volley before the ball hits the side wall. (c)   Volley after the ball hits the side wall. (d)   Drive before the ball hits the back wall. (e)   Drive after the ball hits the back wall. (f)   Boast out of the back corner. (g)   The receiver circles towards the T (anti-clockwise). (h)   The receiver regains the T, which is the first objective in nullifying the server's advantage.

(a)

(b)

(c)

direction of serve. Move forward early and volley around the short line before the ball strikes the wall. Even the best servers can lose their rhythm and confidence under pressure.

Summary

Serving

1.   Take your time and your opportunity.
2.   Have two basic serves that are secure.
3.   Do look at the receiver and tailor your serve accordingly.
4.   Vary the pace and angle of your basic serve.
5.   Put the receiver's high backhand volley to the test.
6.   Don't give him a free volley.
7.   Make hitting the side wall your priority.
8.   Unsettle the receiver with a variety of serves.
9.   As soon as you have served, step on to the T.
10.   Be prepared for the intercepting volley.

STAR TIP

The most important thing I ever tell anyone is, 'Never stop learning', because that's when the pleasure goes away.
Hiddy Jahan

Receiving a Serve

1.   Be patient. Remember, only you can lose the point.
2.   Watch the serve and follow the ball in flight.
3.   Adopt an open-chested stance.
4.   Don't turn. Back off into centre court instead.
5.   Don't get caught flat-footed. Use your feet.
6.   Don't allow the server to settle into a rhythm.
7   Concentrate upon good length and width.
8.   Regain command of the T.
9.   Volley whenever possible.
10.   Vary your returns.

(d)

(e)

(f)

(g)

(h)

PART 2
STROKES

CHAPTER 4

KEEPING IT DEEP

When Jonah Barrington first met his future coach, Nasrullah Khan, he explained that he desperately wanted to become a better squash player.

Nashrullah listened to him with great patience, and then replied quietly:

Everyday you must hit the ball up one side wall a hundred times. This very good thing. Then you hit the ball up other side wall a hundred times. This very good thing, very good practice. This will make you very good squash player.

It was not quite the advice that Barrington, then in his embryo days, had been expecting. However, as the years rolled by, he came to realize that this was in fact very good advice indeed.

Nasrullah, then possibly the best coach in Britain, was simply telling him to concentrate upon the most basic skill in the game. The ability to drive to a length on either wing, while keeping the ball tight.

Squash is a hard-driving game. How well you cover the court and how well you drive sets your standard as a player. There is room for all sorts of players – power players, shot players, runners, volleyers, lob and drop merchants, and deceptive players – but they must all have the ability to drive to a length.

It is the bread-and-butter shot, if you like; without it, your game will suffer the same fate as a house with weak foundations: it will crumble.

Unfortunately, defence is a word with a boring connotation. In other sports, it conjures up images of ten-man rugby, Catenaccio and Barnacle Bailey. However, in squash, it is a little different. Defence is the base upon which attacking squash is built, and certainly it is the key to success.

Barrington, when he eventually became the world number one, was the classic example. He based his entire approach upon (in his own words) 'burying my opponent in the back corners'.

The three shots which can achieve this are the straight drive, the crosscourt drive and the lob. These are the three pillars of the defensive game.

The Straight Drive

This is the tightest shot in squash and, therefore, the most difficult to attack. It is always a good notion to have a picture of perfection in your mind. The perfect straight drive would be so tight that it would cling or roll along the side wall, and then die on the second bounce in the back-wall nick. That is the ideal and if you can learn to do that every time, Jahangir will soon be trembling at the very mention of your name. Anyway, this is the target you should be trying to achieve . . .

Remember that good length and good width are the key elements to a drive. The beauty about a really tight drive is that it is virtually impregnable against attack, and at the same time, capable of putting your opponent into deep trouble. If not an outright winner, it should pave the way for a winner to be hit from the scrambled return.

Technique

For a straight forehand drive, face the side wall with the leading shoulder pointing into the front right-hand corner. The leading foot (the left) points towards the place where the ball should bounce, about 1 m (3ft) away. You then strike the ball as it crosses that imaginary line. The impact will occur about a racket's length in front of that left foot. If you wish to angle the ball in for good width, let it come back a little more.

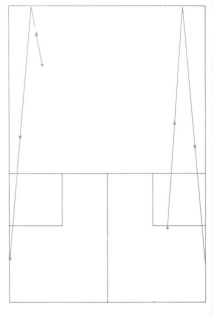

Fig 31   The straight drive placement. Angle the ball so that it will make contact with the side wall just behind the service box.

For a straight backhand drive, everything is the same apart from the impact point. This time, you strike the ball 30cm (1ft) before it reaches the leading foot.

As you swing, your weight moves

evenly from the back foot to the front foot. Remember to keep the head still, very much like a golfer. The shoulders should remain parallel to the side wall.

The Crosscourt Drive

Abou Taleb described the crosscourt drive as a 'good friend and a bad enemy'. This was his way of saying that, despite its undoubted value, it can be a risky shot unless played well and at the right moment.

> **STAR TIP**
>
> *The crosscourt is a good friend and a bad enemy.*
>
> Abou Taleb

The advantage of a well played crosscourt is that the ball runs across the backwall, rather than rebounding forward, as with the straight drive. However, a loose crosscourt, shoulder high and through the middle of the court, will be cannon fodder for experienced volleyers.

Therefore, you need to be very precise when playing crosscourts and very selective. Err on the side of caution. If in doubt, play straight.

All the problems stem from the fact that the shot does not have the constant protection of the side and back walls that is enjoyed by the straight drive. On its flight across the open court, it is vulnerable. This is why the angle is all important. Often when I am playing with a pupil who hits a loose crosscourt I will stop the game, and hold my racket out sideways to show how much of the court is being covered. Then I will ask him to point out the spot on the side wall which should have been his target. To achieve maximum width, this should be the spot immediately level with the opponent. And if the opponent was on the T, that spot would be around the back of the service box.

Despite the risks, the crosscourt does have several technical advantages:

Fig 32   The classic backhand drive as demonstrated by Jahangir. Del Harris, poised and watchful on the T.

Figs 33 (a)–(f)　The straight forehand drive.

Figs 33 (a)–(f)　The arm is bent at the top of the backswing, straight on impact and then bends again after the follow through. Note how the body is balanced throughout the swing, and how the weight is transferred on to the leading foot at the moment of impact.

(a)

(b)

(c)

(d)

(e)

(f)

Figs 34 (a)–(f)   The straight backhand drive.

(a)

Figs 34 (a)–(f)   The swing is similar to that of the forehand drive, but tends to be more fluent, as (with the body out of the way) the arm can flow freely. Note the ball is taken earlier, about 30cm (1ft) in front of the leading foot.

(b)

(c)

(d)

(e)

(f)

Figs 35 (a)–(f)　The crosscourt drive.

Figs 35 (a)–(f)　*The ball is taken much earlier than in either of the straight drives, ideally when it is opposite the leading knee. Note the open stance and the stillness of the head and shoulders.*

(a)

(b)

(c)

(d)

(e)

(f)

1.   There is always the possibility of a side-wall nick.

2.   Due to its sideways path, it is also likely to die against the back wall.

3.   Once an opponent has been passed, he will be forced to turn and chase.

4.   Due to its longer path, you have more time in which to regain the T.

Ideally, crosscourts should be hit from the front or middle of the court when your opponent is out of position. This gives you a better chance of beating his volley. However, I sometimes use it as a surprise shot when I am behind my opponent. A lot of players become disorientated when the ball is fired past them in this way.

Technique

This time, we run much more directly towards the ball, but still slightly to one side. The open stance (described in Chapter 2) is the recommended one, as the ball has to be played in front of the body. To make interception more unlikely, vary the height, pace, length and width of your shots.

The Lob

The lob is the most underrated and under-used shot in squash. For those of us fortunate enough to have watched Gogi Alauddin, the arch exponent of the lob, it is hard to understand why. As he demonstrated so vividly, it has a multitude of uses.

Primarily, it is a defensive shot, used to buy time when you are under pressure at the front of the court, enabling you to regain the T and the initiative.

It can be used to slow the pace of a

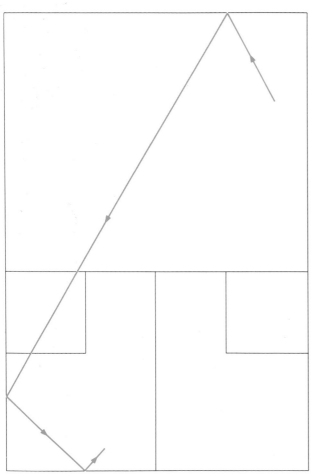

Fig 36 (a)   The crosscourt drive. Angle the ball to make contact with the side wall on the full just behind the service box, and then hit the floor and back wall – in that order.

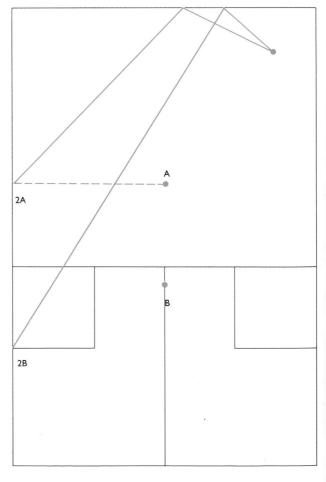

Fig 36 (b)   With the crosscourt, the need to pass your opponent is paramount. To achieve the necessary width, aim to hit the side wall level with your opponent. As with opponent A, 2A becomes your target; with opponent B, it is 2B.

Fig 37 The high backswing of Ross Norman in action against Rodney Eyles. No one takes the racket through a wider arc than the New Zealander.

Figs 38 (a)–(e)   The crosscourt lob.

Figs 38 (a)–(e)   The face of the racket is kept very open to achieve the height that this shot needs. The body is low and the final stride long. For perfection, the lob needs to satisfy the three dimensions – height, width and length.

(a)

(b)

(c)

(d)

(e)

Figs 39 (a)–(c)   Lobbing when scrambling.

(a)

(b)

Figs 39 (a)–(c)   You are scrambling to reach the ball close to the front wall. Your opponent is behind you, but you are not quite sure where. At such times, the lob has to be your escape shot. Therefore, concentrate upon getting your racket under the ball and lifting it high on to the front wall. Bend the knees, stretch the legs, and get as low as possible, without sacrificing balance.

(c)

game when you become tired or temporarily in oxygen debt; to disturb your opponent's rhythm; or to exploit any weakness he may have on the volley. When played with the touch of an artist, it can be a winner, hanging in the air and falling almost vertically to die in the back corners.

The lob is at its most effective on a cold court and is normally played crosscourt. However, the straight lob can be almost equally effective, although it carries the greater risk of catching the wall above the out-of-court line.

Targets

When playing the crosscourt lob, you can have a variety of targets:

1.   You can play it like the semi-lob serve, targeted to hit the side wall high up behind the service box. Keep it 60cm (2ft) below the out-of-court line, so that you have a reasonable margin for error.
2.   You can toss up a very high lob, designed to fall into the back corner.
3.   If under severe pressure, you can again toss it up high so that it strikes the back wall on the full and then angles in towards the side wall.

KEY POINT

To improve length when playing from the back court, hit well above the cut line. The further you are from the front wall, the higher you aim.

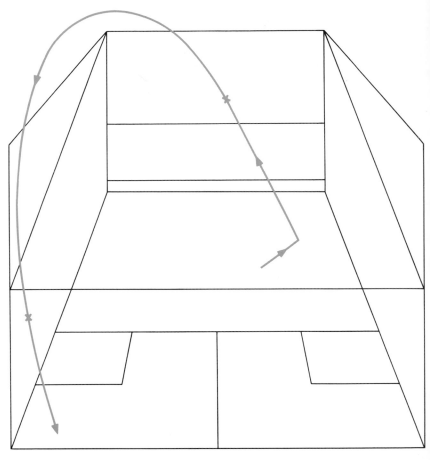

Fig 40   The crosscourt lob. Height, width and length are the key elements in this shot. The ball should be high enough to clear your opponent in mid-court; wide and tight enough to make volleying difficult; and deep enough to pose problems if it hits the floor.

Technique

Use the open stance for the crosscourt lob and bend your knees so that you get down low. You need to get under the ball with a very open racket face. Stroke smoothly down, under and up on the ball. Get a sharp angle and make contact high above the cut line. This is best described as a scooped shot, gentle yet firm, and heeding all three dimensions – height, length and width. Always bear in mind that the lob must clear both your opponent and his outstretched racket.

When playing the straight lob, revert to the normal forehand footwork (as in the drive) and beware of that out-of-court line.

Summary

1.   The straight drive is the bread-and-butter shot in squash, and the key one.
2.   Bury your opponent in the back corners.
3.   Keep the straight drive so tight that it is impregnable against attack.
4.   Keep your basic game as straight as possible.
5.   Err on the side of caution.
6.   Use width to beat the volley when hitting crosscourt.
7.   Use the crosscourt sparingly.
8.   Use the lob to buy time when you are out of position.
9.   Use the lob to disturb your opponent's rhythm.
10.   Use the lob to exploit any weakness your opponent may have overhead.

CHAPTER 5

POURING ON THE PRESSURE

Hashim Khan, the best player of his day (some say of any day) always preached the gospel of 'maximum pressure with minimum risk'. This was the message he gave daily to his two star pupils, his brother Azam and cousin Mohibullah, who both underlined it by becoming British Open champions.

Today, it is still the maxim we all try to follow. For squash is a pressure game. Just about anyone can look reasonably impressive on court, if given the time to play their shots in a leisurely way, so do not allow your opponent such luxuries.

Deprive him of time, make him run as perhaps he has never had to run before, force him to scrape up his returns at full stretch, and pressurize him into mistakes.

The two key shots in the pressure game are the volleys and the hard drives.

The Volley

Qamar Zaman, one of the great touch players of our time, once said, 'A man who doesn't volley has only one reason for playing squash. That is to do a lot of running and lose weight'.

Now Zaman is a whimsical fellow and so this perhaps needs a word of explanation. It is not meant to imply that

the volleyer stands still and his opponent does all the running. You need to be very fit to 'hunt the ball' in the way the top players do.

Nevertheless, a great master of the art like Zaman will spend more time on the T than most and it is rare to see him scurrying into the back corners, simply because he will normally have cut off the ball in flight.

There are a whole range of volleys, and this is a word that can be thought of more as an adjective than a noun. You can have a volley drive (or drive volley if you wish), a volley drop, a volley boast and even a volley lob – a shot that Lisa Opie has played to perfection against her great rival, the much taller Martine Le Moignan.

If you wish to dominate the T, the volley has to be one of your chief weapons. For so many of the loose shots which can be intercepted will be coming through that area, and a good volleyer will be able to stay there for long spells, while stretching his opponent to the limit.

Technique

The basic volley is not a kill shot. It is played parallel to the floor like a normal drive and targeted for the back of the service box. We use a much shorter swing than normal and a punching action,

because time is often short when volleying.

For the same reason, it is not always possible to get the feet right. But we should still try to turn the shoulders, so that we are facing the wall. The ball should be struck well in front of the leading shoulder and aimed above the cut line with an open racket face. The wrist action is locked.

With a hard crosscourt volley, aim for the nick behind the service box. Get good width on all your crosscourt volleys, otherwise the tables could be turned. Your opponent could intercept and become the volleyer.

Figs 41 (a)–(f)   The high volley.

Figs 41 (a)–(f)   Punch through the ball striking it with an open racket. Note that the wrist is firm and contact made opposite the leading shoulder.

(a)

(b)

(c)

(d)

(e)

(f)

Figs 42 (a)–(e)   The drop volley.

Figs 42 (a)–(e)   This is sometimes called a stop volley and this describes the shot well. The racket face is tilted to aim the ball towards the desired spot in the corner, and the follow-through is less pronounced than with the normal drop. The aim is to take all the original pace off the ball, so that it will die quickly.

(a)

(b)

(c)

(d)

(e)

Figs 43 (a)–(c)   Volleying the bodyline ball.

(a)   *(b)*   *(c)*

Figs 43 (a)–(c)   There will be times when the ball has been fired straight at you and you won't be able to adjust your feet. Therefore, improvise; step sideways and turn your hips so that your body is half-facing the side wall. Shorten your backswing and punch the ball. The arc of your hand will be very small, so you will have to rely upon power from your forearm and wrist.

The Hard Drive

The hard, low drive is all about pace. It is the sheer pace of the ball that pressurizes your opponent by denying him the time he would wish to have. Drive to a dying length, forcing him to take the ball before it reaches the back wall. If you are crosscourting, again hit hard and low and go for a dying width.

To increase the pressure, it is important to move swiftly and take the ball early. However, this does have in-built dangers. In a bid to harry their opponents, many players are apt to harry themselves, and consequently lose control, play loose shots or, even worse, hit into the tin.

Don't try to take the cover off every ball. It is much wiser to maintain a balance.

Game, Set and Tie

Mike Corby had arrived at the RAC Club to play in the British Open, only to find his path barred by a uniformed doorman. 'I'm afraid, sir,' said the doorman, 'you can't come into the club dressed like that. You must first put on a tie'. Corby was already late for his match and in no mood to argue. He side-stepped and sprinted down the corridor with the doorman in pursuit, but losing ground. As a result of this episode, Corby was subsequently banned from the club for breaking the dress regulations. A few years later, he returned for another British Open, this time correctly attired. He then stepped on court wearing his normal squash kit, plus a white silk tie.

Decide when you want to go for position and when for pace. Alternate good length with dying length. This way the pressure drive maintains an element of surprise and is, therefore, much more effective.

No one has a monopoly on pressure, so it is reasonable to assume that your opponent will be trying to do to you what you are doing to him. When this happens, move back into your defensive game. Be adaptable; when the situation changes, be prepared to change your game instantly.

If forced to scramble at the front, throw up a lob – buying yourself time to regain the T – then once again start looking for opportunities to pressurize your opponent.

Remember your basic tactical plan. First,

Fig 44 The power-play of Susan Devoy. This is another reason why she has been so dominant in the women's game.

Fig 46   This is the sort of pressure Jahangir can put you under. But the athletic Maclean still gets to the ball. Big question: will he have time to regain the T?

you play a tight defensive game, designed to pin your opponent into the back corners and give you command of the T. Then you look for the chance to apply pressure (the second phase) in a bid to force an error or at least a loose shot. And when that happens, you move on to the attack (the third phase) which, by an odd coincidence, happens to be the title of our next chapter.

Summary

1.   Seek to deprive your opponent of time.
2.   Increase pressure by taking the ball early.
3.   Learn to hunt the ball.
4.   Volley to cut off shots aimed for the back corners.
5.   Pressurize your opponent into errors.
6.   Use early racket preparation when volleying.
7.   Volley in order to gain command of the T.
8.   Vary good length with dying length for your hard drives.
9.   Volley with a short, punching action.
10.   Be prepared to switch from the pressure game to the defensive game, and back again.

Fig 45   The disappearing racket of Eric Sommers. Just once in a while, the speed of the hand defeats the camera.

CHAPTER 6

ON TO THE ATTACK

A young batsman had just returned to the Lords dressing-room in deep gloom. At a crucial stage in the match, he had been caught on the square leg boundary off a long hop.

Denis Compton, hero of a bygone age, patted him kindly on the shoulder. 'Don't worry,' he said, 'it was still the right shot. When the bad balls come, you've got to attack them. Otherwise, what's the point of playing?'

It is a sentiment dear to my own heart. In squash, the defensive and pressure phases are designed to set up winning opportunities, and these must be taken. Otherwise (as the man says) what is the point of playing?

However, it is important to recognize these opportunities and not to simply attack every ball regardless. The correct choice of shots is so crucial in squash.

It is time to attack when you have two conditions in your favour:

1. An easy ball.
2. An opponent out of position.

The main bastions of the attacking game are the drop, the front-court angles, the attacking volleys and the stun drives.

The Odd Drop

Fran Marshall, a former Scottish ladies champion with an adventurous nature, lived much of her life in Kenya. She once arrived at a squash club, limping heavily. Her opponent enquired about the injury. 'I was riding and I fell off,' replied the adventurous lady. She was asked about the horse. 'Oh, it wasn't a horse,' replied Fran matter-of-factly, 'It was a rhino'.

The Drop

Susan Devoy's backhand drop is probably the most feared shot in women's squash. Opponents will sometimes base their tactics on a forehand game just to keep her away from that deadly wing and that deadly shot.

This is some indication of how effective the drop can be when played by an artist, and it does have an undeniable appeal, being very much the favourite of the connoisseur. Hashim once described it as 'the most important shot in the game'. There may be some debate about that, but I understand what he meant. No one can ever claim to be a squash master until he or she has first mastered the drop.

However, it is a high-risk shot: a fraction too low and you will hit tin; a fraction too high and too angled, and it will be a gift for a fleet-footed opponent.

Therefore, make sure you get the right balance between winners and mistakes. In squash, like all other competitive sports, you need to study the percentages.

If your drops have already produced a few winners in any given match, do not make the mistake of overdoing them, of becoming readable and predictable. The drop is ideally a surprise shot. Try to keep it that way.

For this reason, I treat it as a dummy drive. By using the same high backswing (as for the drive), I aim to keep my opponent back behind the short line.

This is a delicate, precise shot and, therefore, not a shot to play when you are under pressure. Employ it only when you are in control of the rally, ideally when your opponent is out of position and too deep. It is the classic reply to the back-corner boast, because it forces your opponent to run the length of the diagonal.

Look upon it as a three-purpose shot:

KEY POINT

When attempting to hit harder, many players rotate their shoulders. This is a body fault and usually results in an inability to hit straight.

1. It can be an outright winner when played into the nick or left tight against the side wall.
2. It can pave the way for a winning shot when your opponent has to scramble to reach it. If you are in position to volley his weak return, that should be the rally's end.
3. It can force your opponent to cover more ground than he would wish, and so sap his stamina.

Technique

Continue to regard the drop as a dummy drive, so the feet are positioned as though for the drive (whether straight or crosscourt) and the backswing is also the same. However, the downswing slows down rather than speeds up through the hitting area.

The racket face on contact is almost horizontal. I like to feel as though I am catching the ball on my racket. I then strike through the ball, letting the racket strings impart the necessary cut. The ball remains in contact with the strings for longer than on any other shot.

Pakistan players such as Zaman have mastered the art of cut to such a degree that many of their drops appear to die almost as soon as they touch the floor. By

Fig 47   Susan Devoy plays a backhand drop from the short line. This is the most feared shot in women's squash. Liz Irving will need all her pace to reach it.

Figs 48 (a)–(e)   The straight forehand drop.

Figs 48 (a)–(e)   Remember to adopt the same backswing as in the straight drive to disguise your intentions. The racket slows (rather than accelerates) during the swing. Note the very open racket face and the shorter follow through.

KEY POINT

When playing the drop, many players place too much emphasis upon perfection and pay the price. Play the percentages, go for a 'working' drop that hits the front wall several centimetres above the tin and then bounces on the floor first – close to the side wall, but not necessarily in the nick.

(a)

(b)

Figs 49 (a)–(f)   The straight backhand drop.

Figs 49 (a)–(f)   For true artists such as Susan Devoy, this is the favoured side. The secret of this shot is to cut the strings down the back of the ball, encouraging it to die quickly. A gentle touch and a very open racket will achieve this aim. Hiddy Jahan demonstrates.

(a)

(b)

(c)

(c)

(d)

(e)

(d)

(e)

(f)

Figs 50 (a)–(e)   The crosscourt drop.

Figs 50 (a)–(e)   Like all crosscourt shots, the ball is taken earlier than in the straight version. Ideally played when the ball is in the front of the court and can therefore be stroked across the face of the front wall to die in the far corner.

(a)

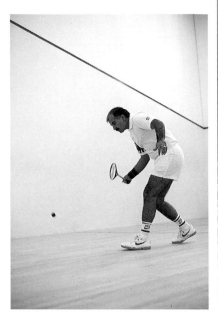

(b)

(c)

(d)

(e)

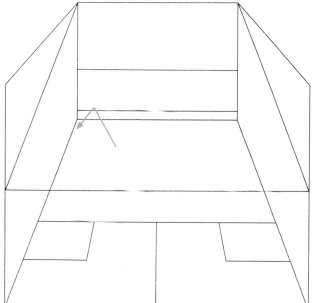

Fig 51 The straight drop. Make sure that the ball's flight is a gentle arc, rather than a flat path. It stays much tighter that way.

Fig 52 The crosscourt drop. It is important that the ball shouldn't hit the opposite wall on the full. Ideally, it should hit the floor first and then die against the wall, or land directly in the nick.

contrast, most of the top Egyptian players down the years have preferred to rely upon softness of touch – in their case merely a caress.

One of the secrets of playing the drop well is to let the hand guide the racket and pace the shot.

Many players make the mistake of stabbing at the ball. The drop does need a full follow-through, however gentle. You can liken it in many ways to a golfer's putt. A staccato stab on the green would be disastrous too.

A good drop should not bounce too far from the front wall and should be aimed to either hit the nick or low down on the side wall. Make sure that it always touches two walls before it reaches the floor. This reduces the speed and consequently the bounce.

Do remember to cover your shot; do not assume that the rally is over. Get back to the T-area, using that L-shaped curve. This is important, because so many good drops have been wasted by the striker's slowness to move. The cost is counted in lets and strokes.

One final tip: play your drop high enough above the tin to give a reasonable margin for error. How high do you need to aim to get nine out of ten?

The Boast

In this instance, we are referring to the front-court angle, the attacking version of the boast. This is the great moving shot. Use it to move the ball away from your opponent. Push him deep, wait for the short ball and boast. Follow up and look for the volley. Try to move your opponent up and down the court, rather than from side to side.

The three-wall boast targeted for the nick on the opposite side wall is a spectacular winner when it works. The shot can also be effective when it strikes that wall just above the floor. The three walls will have put so much spin on the ball that it will die quickly.

However, unless you have devoted countless hours of practice to it, this is an unnecessarily risky shot. The slightest miscalculation will present your opponent with an easy mid-court shot. Therefore,

I suggest that you concentrate on the more gentle two-wall boast, endeavouring to get the second bounce to die in the nick. This is a much better percentage shot.

Technique

Take up the basic stance, as though about to play a normal straight drive. Only this time, let the ball come between you and the side wall before making contact. Stroke smoothly, and then vary the angles and the height, so that you can get the ball to die close to the opposite side wall.

Attacking Volleys

Much of the pressure and attacking play of the modern game is based on the volley. Make sure it becomes part of your game. Always be on the look out for chances to volley and, like the top professionals, learn to hunt the ball. Remember that all the shots mentioned in this chapter can be volleyed, and if volleyed correctly, they should prove even more effective, simply because they have stolen that vital bit of time.

The Stun Drive

This is the ultimate aggressive shot in squash. A sophisticated shot played from the front of the court and only just above the tin. Even the very best of players give themselves a margin of error on this one.

The opportunity to play this shot comes when your opponent has played a loose ball into the front half of the court, away from the side wall and bouncing above the height of the tin. The height of the bounce is vital, because to kill the ball you have to hit down, so unless the ball is at least 60cm (2ft) above the floor, there is clearly a danger of rattling the tin which is 48cm (19in) high.

Fig 53   Del Harris in action against Rodney Martin – stretched, but perfectly balanced.

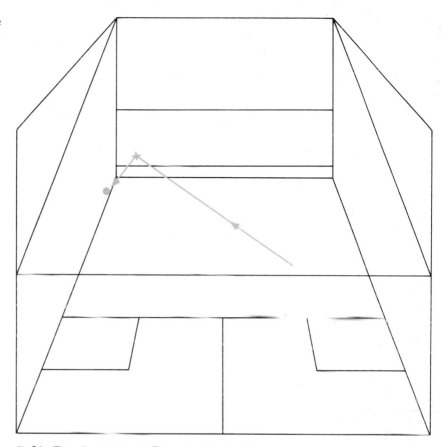

Fig 51   The volley into the nick. The most aggressive shot in squash and one that needs much practice before being employed in a match. Use a punching action.

Struck correctly, the stun drive engenders so much pace and so much backspin that your opponent will need to get to the ball very quickly indeed. Such a shot would bounce twice before it reached the short line.

Technique

Look upon the shot as simply a very violent form of the normal drive and, therefore, adopt the basic stance for the straight stun drive and the open stance for the crosscourt version.

Use an open racket face (vital for this shot) and hit down, heavily cutting the ball. It is the speed of the racket head and the open face that combines to make this such an aggressive shot.

Set out to make your attacking game as varied and unpredictable as possible. If squash is a form of battle, shots are your weapons. The more you have in your armoury, the more successful you are likely to be.

Figs 55 (a)–(c)   Volley into the nick.

(a)

Figs 55 (a)–(c)   This is the most spectacular shot in squash with a high-risk factor. The aim is to strike the ball hard and with a downward trajectory, so that it hits just above the tin and dies in the side-wall nick. Note that despite the downward trajectory, the racket face has remained open.

(b)

(c)

Figs 56 (a)–(c)   The stun drive.

(a)

Figs 56 (a)–(c)   Strike the ball when it is high above the tin. This is important, because you are hitting it down. The aim is to cut the ball so heavily that it will bounce twice before it reaches the short line. Racket-head speed and an open face are the keys to a successful stun drive.

(b)

(c)

Figs 57 (a)–(e)   The trickle boast.

Figs 57 (a)–(e)   Like the drop, this shot is disguised as a dummy drive with a normal backswing. Note how at the last moment before impact, the racket face turns, striking the ball gently into the side wall. An open face and a gentle touch are the keys to a successful trickle boast. The head looks at the front wall, encouraging the opponent to expect a shot down the wall.

(a)

(b)

(c)

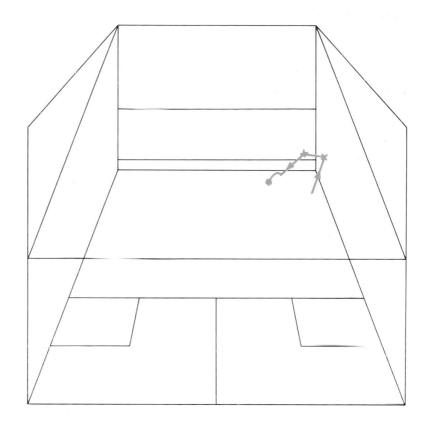

Fig 58   The trickle boast. The ball is played flat just above the tin, so that it will bounce as quickly as possible.

This can be played as a useful alternative to the drop. This is a shot to be played when the ball is in the front of the court and close to one of the walls. Shape up as though about to play a straight drive, but take the ball later than normal. Then, just before impact, turn the face of the racket towards the wall. Ideally, the ball should stay close to the front wall and die against the far wall. To be successful, this has to be a gentle shot.

KEY POINT

Aim to play your winners from the front of the court, and whether the shot happens to be a drop, trickle boast or kill, be sure you can cover it.

(e)

Figs 59 (a)–(e)   The reverse angle.

Figs 59 (a)–(e)   This is essentially a surprise shot, ideally played when an opponent has hit a loose crosscourt from the back and failed to regain the T. Therefore, as in this sequence, the striker masks the ball with his body and makes much use of his wrist. This shot is normally played from the front of the court.

(a)

(b)

(c)

(d)

(e)

The Three-Wall Boast

This is aimed directly for the nick and is too risky (as I suggested) for a conventional shot, but it can nevertheless be used as a variation. It does need a lot of practice, because you need to be accurate.

The Reverse Angle

This is one of the major surprise shots and is normally heavily disguised. Adopt an open stance and take the ball early as you would for a crosscourt. Aim the ball at such an angle that it strikes the far wall, makes contact just above the tin, stays close to the front wall and dies close to the near wall.

Ideally, it is a shot to be played in the front of the court, when your opponent is out of position and trapped behind you, on the opposite side to the ball's final destination. The reverse angle is often disguised as a crosscourt drive. Just once in a while, I like to play it from behind my opponent to disorientate him, but only once in a while.

KEY POINT

A ball in the front that hits the side wall on the full will bounce out into court. So if you wish to keep the ball tight, make sure it hits the floor first.

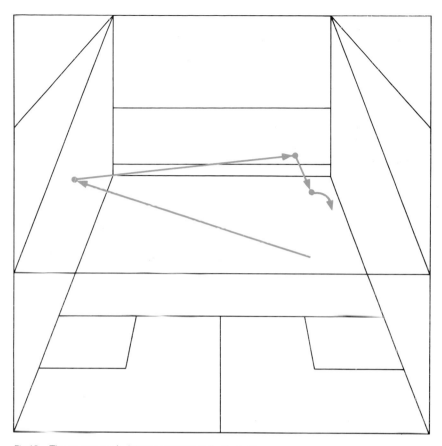

Fig 60 The reverse angle. It is important to strike the ball in front of your body, and to angle it to stay tight in the front of the court.

Summary

1. When the opportunity to attack comes, take it.
2. Attack when you have an easy ball.
3. Attack when your opponent is out of position.
4. Regard the drop as a dummy drive.
5. Don't let your drop become predictable.
6. Move your opponent with the boast.
7. The two-wall boast (as opposed to three wall) is the percentage shot.
8. Don't attempt a stun drive unless the bounce is at least 60cm (2ft) high.
9. Always allow yourself a margin for error.

KEY POINT

When playing the hard low drive, increase the speed of the racket head. Punch through the ball on impact.

---

10. Introduce as many variations as possible into your game.

CHAPTER 7

THE GRAVEYARD

The back of a squash court is sometimes described as the 'graveyard', because this is the area in which so many dreams have foundered and died.

The first problem for a beginner is that of putting the ball into the back corners. The second is that of getting it out. For it is very possible that your opponent (the dirty dog) will be doing to you what you are trying so hard to do to him, and it is never quite enough, just to get the ball out of those corners.

The important thing is really how well and how tight you can play your shot. Your future as a squash player depends to a large extent upon your ability to get the ball into and out of the back corners.

One of the main reasons why Geoff Hunt came to dominate squash was because of his back-corner skills. No one ever played the back corners better than this eight-times British Open champion and the truth is that he needed to do so, for it can be no coincidence that his great rival, Jonah Barrington, was the leading exponent of the art of 'burying' his opponents in the corners.

The three standard shots to be played

from this position are the straight drive, the boast and the crosscourt drive. However, given the choice, the favourite has to be the straight drive, because it is the tight shot of the trio.

The Straight Drive

The Situation

Your opponent has put you into the back forehand corner and is anticipating a weak drive which he will be able to intercept and attack. You want to reverse the situation, i.e. to put your opponent into the corner and yourself back in the T.

The Solution

Position well to the side of the ball, so that you will be able to get the racket behind and under it. Use a compact swing and a very open racket face. Aim high above the cut line, bringing the ball back to land just behind the service box. Keep it tight to the wall (a clinger if possible). Don't give him anything to attack.

Improvise

If the ball is really tight in that corner, you may well have to improvise. Don't adopt the conventional back-corner stance; instead lead with the 'wrong' foot, i.e. the right (see Chapter 2, page 24). Slide your hand up the handle, so that your racket will not make contact with the back wall, and use more wrist to accelerate and lift the ball.

Note The change of stance only applies to the forehand. On the backhand, the back-corner stance does not pose any problems.

> **KEY POINT**
>
> When playing a back-corner boast, beware of two common failings:
>
> 1. In a bid for greater power, don't close the racket face. Keep it open, so that the ball travels upwards.
> 2. In a bid to direct the ball towards the front wall, don't rotate the shoulders. Play the shot like a normal drive.

The Back-Corner Boast

Geoff Hunt once advised, 'Consider carefully playing a boast, then don't'. This is because the back-corner boast is a last-resort shot, one that your opponent should reach with some ease from the T, and one that he is likely to drop, forcing you to run the diagonal.

The Situation

Your opponent has passed you down the wall, so you are arriving late in the corner

> **KEY POINT**
>
> Don't try to hit the ball hard from a tight back-corner position. There isn't enough room for a full swing. So float the ball gently; and by so doing, buy the time you need to regain the T.
>
> Only play the hard, flat boast if your opponent is:
>
> 1. A front-wall watcher.
> 2. Out of position.
> 3. Desperately slow.

Fig 61   Mir Zaman straightens the ball out of a back corner. Notice the feet.

Figs 62 (a)–(f)   The back-corner boast.

Figs 62 (a)–(f)   Adopt a back-corner stance, toes pointing into the corner and knees bent. The swing is the same as that for the drive. Keep the face of the racket open; and remember to boast (or boost) the ball upwards, aiming to strike the side wall above an imaginary tin.

(a)

(b)

(c)

(d)

(e)

(f)

and this time there is no chance of playing straight. Your opponent knows you will have to boast and is planning a quick drop, which will stretch you over the diagonal. Your aim for the moment is simply that of keeping the rally alive.

The Solution

An optimist or a Jansher might go for a dead nick, but much wiser is to float your boast. Instead of hitting the ball low and hard over the tin, play a higher and gentler shot. This will remain longer in flight and thus give you the time you need to regain the T. The ball should bounce in the opposite front corner, while slowing and moving in towards the far wall.

The word 'boast' is said to have been derived from 'boost', and this gives a clear reminder as to how the shot should be played. Because of its flight pattern, the ball needs to be boosted upwards. Remember that and it will prevent a lot of balls hitting tin. Adopt the back-corner stance.

The Skid Boast

The Situation

You have once more been passed by your opponent and again it is going to be difficult to straighten the ball out of the corner. Your opponent is so convinced that you are about to play a normal back-corner boast that he has moved to the front of the T-area, ready to move fast and play a winning drop. You have no wish to co-operate. Moreover you want to take advantage of the fact that he is out of position if you can conjure up a back-court shot.

The Solution

Play a skid boast. This shot sends the ball high into the side wall and much nearer the front of the court. It then rebounds on to the top quarter of the front wall. From that moment, it behaves like a diagonal lob. The ball should clear your opponent comfortably and make contact with the wall at the back of the service box. It is

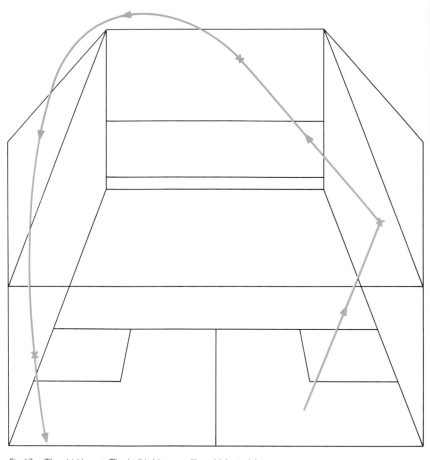

Fig 63   The skid boast. The ball is hit more like a high straight drive than a boast, and then after striking the front wall, it behaves like a heavily cut crosscourt lob. Height is all important.

essential that you follow through with a very open face. On the forehand side only, lead with the wrong foot. This can be an effective shot if used sparingly.

The Back-Wall Boast

The Situation

You have been passed by a ball that threatens to die on the back wall. Your time has run out and you have no chance of getting alongside the ball (let alone behind it). You just want to keep the rally alive.

The Solution

Play a back-wall boast: strike the ball upwards on to the back wall to produce a lob effect, albeit in reverse. All boasts need to be hit upwards, but none more so than this. It is the ultimate last-resort shot, but if played as a high, diagonal lob, it can be a little better than that. It should finish tight against the side wall. Due to its high flight, it will give you time to regain the T.

STAR TIP

If you wish to command the T, play straight and tight.
Nasrullah Khan

Figs 64 (a)–(c) The skid boast.

Figs 64 (a)–(c) This is often played as
an alternative to the back-corner
boast. Contact on the side wall is
much higher and further forward,
hitting a spot which is approximately
half-way between the short line and
the front wall. After rebounding on to
the front wall, the skid boast behaves
like a heavily cut diagonal lob. Note
the very open racket face and the
uplift on the follow through.

(a)

(b)

(c)

Figs 65 (a)–(c)   The back-wall boast.

(a)

Figs 65 (a)–(c)   This has been described as the ultimate last-resort shot, but played correctly it is better than that. Treat it as a diagonal lob played against the back wall. Note the very open racket face; for it is essential to get height. The aim: to persuade it to drop and die in the opposite front corner.

(b)

(c)

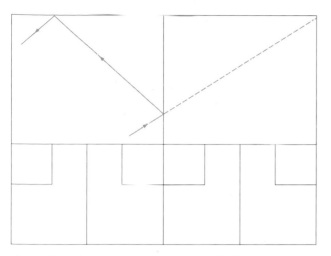

Fig 66 To obtain the correct angle for the boast, it often helps to imagine that you are striking into a transparent wall, and aiming for the far front corner of the adjoining court.

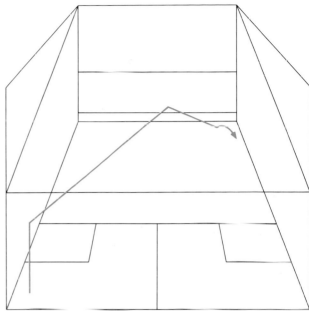

Fig 67 The floated boast. The ball is hit high and lazily on to the side wall with the intention of making it land like a drop shot in the opposite front corner. It should be played as a two-wall boast, not a three-wall.

STAR TIP

Consider carefully playing a boast, then don't

Geoff Hunt

The Crosscourt Drive

The Situation

Your opponent has been playing good length and width and repeatedly putting you into the back corners. With his confidence growing, he has begun to crowd you from the T and fully face the side wall. His aim: to seek more interceptions and increase pressure. Your aim: to dent that confidence and to create enough uncertainty to stop the crowding.

The Solution

Play a crosscourt drive from behind your opponent, aiming for the back of the service box on the far wall. Such a shot will probably disorientate him, as it crosses his body at an unexpected angle on the way to the front wall. It will also place him out of position, facing the wrong wall and with some ground to cover.

Summary

1.   This is a defensive situation, so play safely and patiently.
2.   Your first objective is to reverse the position. Put your opponent in the corner and yourself on the T.
3.   Learn how to straighten the ball out of the corners.
4.   Use a swing that will allow you to get under the ball and lift it.
5.   Given the choice, opt for the straight drive, even if you have to improvize a little.
6.   If forced to boast, make sure you clear the tin.
7.   Play the type of boasts which buy you valuable time.
8.   Employ the back-wall boast with imagination.
9.   Use the crosscourt as a surprise shot

A Promising Beginner

In 1953, Hashim Khan came to Britain to defend his British Open title. He brought with him his younger brother, Azam. 'I would like Azam to play,' said Hashim. 'He only just begun, but one day he be good player.' British officialdom was horrified. 'Sorry old boy,' they said, 'but we can't just let *anyone* play in the Open.' However, to placate Hashim, they gave Azam a trial game against one of Britain's top amateurs, Brian Phillips. Azam won in three without breaking sweat.

That year, Hashim retained his title after a desperately hard-fought five-set final. His opponent in that final: Azam Khan.

to disorientate a confident opponent.
10.   Use variations to break up your opponent's rhythm, but use them sparingly.

PART 3
TACTICS

CHAPTER 8

THE CHOICE OF SHOT

Kevin Shawcross, the former World Amateur Champion from Australia, once outlined his squash philosophy to me thus:

I don't like to do too much rushing around, mate. It gets in the way of my drinking. So when I step on a squash court, I set out to make the other beggars [I think that was the word he used] run as far and as fast as I ruddy well can.

In fact, Kevin, a beer-swilling and very genial giant – 105kg (16½st) in his prime – moved with surprising ease around a squash court. However, that quote summed up what should be the aim of squash players everywhere. Make your opponent do the running. Set out to take his legs away.

To achieve this, you need to make the right choice of shots, and this is a grey area in the game. I estimate that good club players – those on the brink of a county team – probably make the right choice with 80 shots out of every 100 they play. In the middle and lower leagues, the percentage comes down to about 20. So the opportunity for improvement is clearly vast.

The choice will depend upon many factors, including your own ability, your opponent's ability and the state of the match.

It is obviously not very sensible to advise you to play a crosscourt, if width is your weakness and your opponent is a good volleyer; or to suggest a nick, if the only ones you have ever hit surprised you more than anybody else. We must avoid the danger of being too dogmatic.

Still, it will help you to improve this vital aspect of your game if you base your choice of shots on the simple rules that follow.

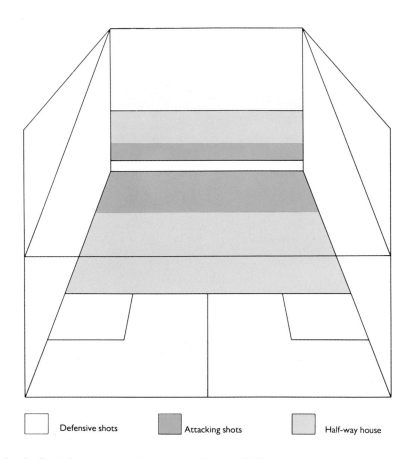

☐ Defensive shots	▨ Attacking shots	☐ Half-way house

Fig 68   The defensive and attacking areas. Use the top half of the front wall for your defensive shots, i.e. the straight drives, crosscourt drives and lobs. Use the lower half for your attacking shots, i.e. the drops, trickle boasts and kills. Avoid the half-way-house zones.

Move your Opponent the Maximum Distance in the Minimum Time

The greatest distances on a squash court are the two diagonals, so have a very clear picture of these in your mind, and stretch your opponent over them whenever possible. Here are some of the shots which will achieve this aim:

1.   *The drop from a back-corner boast.* This is one of the classic moves and has become so widely used that the back-

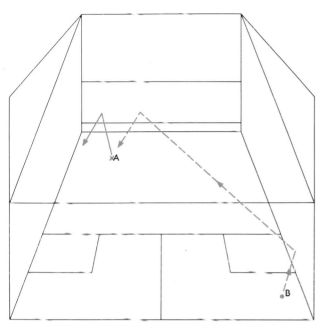

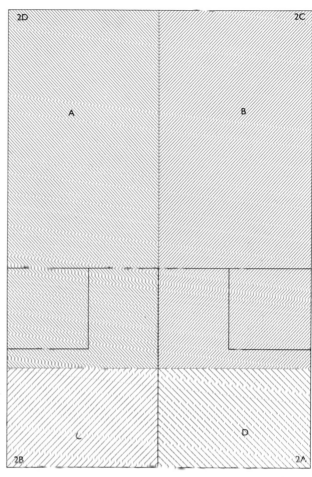

Fig 69   Your opponent has been forced to play a back-corner boast. Counter with a quick drop, thus moving him over the full length of the diagonal.

Fig 70   A basic guide to shot selection, and to the art of moving your opponent the maximum distance in the minimum time. If your opponent is in the area marked A, your shot should finish at point 2A; if in area B, at point 2B; if in area C, at point 2C; if in area D, at point 2D.

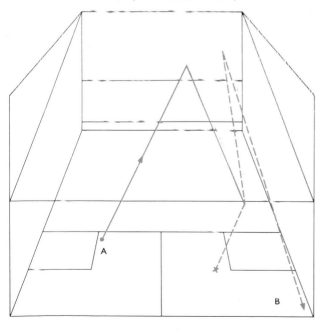

corner boast is now a shot that most players try to avoid. The counter is effective for two reasons: the back-corner boast is an easy shot to anticipate, and is very often the last option, so you can move forward in the T-area, ready for the quick drop; and the back corner is a difficult position from which to regain the T rapidly.

2.   *The attacking angle from a loose straight drive.* Your opponent has managed to straighten the ball out of the back corner, but he has hit it too low on the front wall. One big step from the T will enable you to boast it into the side wall

Fig 71   Your opponent has hit a loose serve, too far from the side wall and coming to you at a comfortable height. Step forward and play a straight volley, taking his time away.

with the opposite front corner as your target.

3. *The crosscourt drop from a loose straight drive.* This is virtually the same situation as the previous one, only this time, the ball is a more comfortable distance from the side wall. The crosscourt drop thus becomes the simpler shot.

4. *The crosscourt lob when your opponent has anticipated a drop.* You have already played several successful drops; and your opponent (anticipating another) is moving towards that front corner. The crosscourt lob will thus take him over the most difficult diagonal. It is always more taxing to move backwards than forwards down a court.

5. *The straight drive from a loose front-court angle.* Your opponent's shot has been hit too high and too sharply on to the front wall, so you intercept and volley straight down the side wall.

6. *The straight drop from a loose crosscourt drive.* Your opponent's shot lacks the width to pass you, so intercept and play a volley drop into the corner.

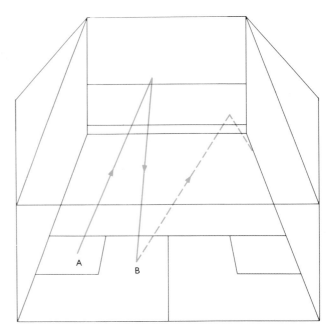

Fig 72   Your opponent has played a loose straight ball. Keep him trapped behind you and play a crosscourt drop, moving him once more over the diagonal.

Fig 73   Your opponent has put you under pressure in the front of the court. He is anticipating a drop and is moving forward to cover that shot. Play a high crosscourt lob which will at the very least force him to turn and hurry.

Fig 74   Your opponent has forced you deep, anticipated a back-corner boast and is already moving forward to cover that shot. Play a skid boast high over his head which (as in Fig 73) will make him turn and hurry.

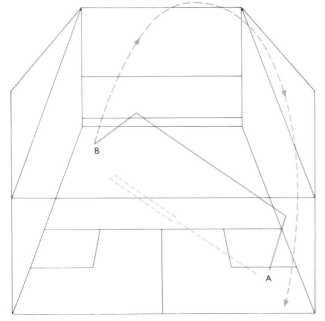

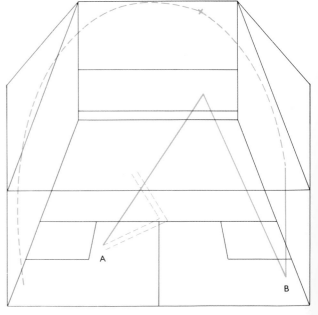

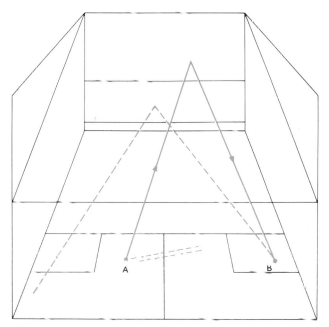

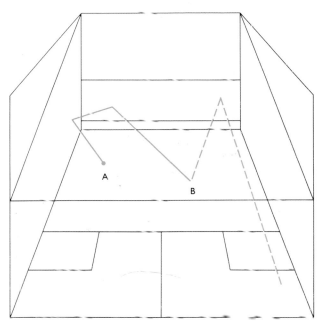

Fig 75   Your opponent (having served) is beginning to crowd you from the T. His hope is that you will play a loose straight drive. Instead, hit a hard, deep crosscourt. In addition to wrong-footing him, it will also stop him crowding you for a while.

Fig 76   Your opponent has played a loose front-court angle, which you can intercept. Straight drive it down the wall. Your opponent, having been deprived of time to regain the T, will thus be forced to once again cover most of the diagonal.

Fig 77   Your opponent has played a poor drop and stayed too far forward in a bid to cover his own shot. Shape for the drop or straight drive, but hit a deep crosscourt.

Fig 78   Your opponent has played another drop and is moving backwards towards the T. While he is still moving, play a drop of your own, hopelessly wrong-footing him.

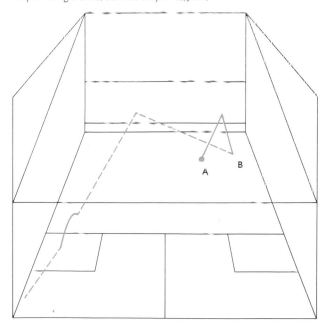

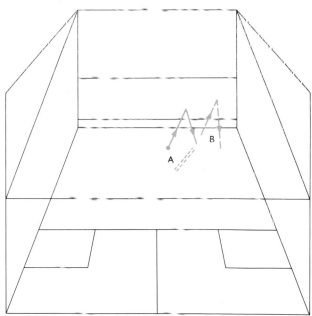

Always Try to Play the Shot that Leaves You on the T

You must always assume that your opponent can return your shot, which

KEY POINT

Remember that the straight shot down the wall has to be your most basic and most used shot. This is the one, more than any other, which helps you to command the T.

means that you must cover it. So when you have been forced out of position, play a shot that will buy you the time you need to regain the T. The following are examples:

1. You are scrambling to reach a ball in the front of the court and doubt that you can hit it past your opponent, so toss up a high lob – preferably a diagonal one, because it has a longer flight path.

2. You are boasting out of a back corner and very much aware that your opponent, who is quick, will be hoping to stretch you with a quick drop. Therefore, float your boast, high and lazy, to gain that extra bit of time you need.

KEY POINT

If your opponent is out of position at the back of the court, the drop will be your best option four times out of five. But still play it as a dummy drive.

Figs 79–88   Shot selection.

(a)

Figs 79 (a) and (b)   A drop, following a back-corner boast.

(b)

(a)

Figs 80 (a) and (b)   A volley boast, following a loose straight drive.

(b)

Figs 81 (a) and (b)   A drop, following a short crosscourt.

(a)

(b)

Figs 82 (a) and (b)   A crosscourt drop, following a loose straight ball.

(a)

(b)

Figs 83 (a) and (b)   A crosscourt lob, when the opponent has anticipated a drop.

(a)

(b)

Figs 84 (a) and (b)   A skid boast, when the opponent has anticipated a back-corner boast.

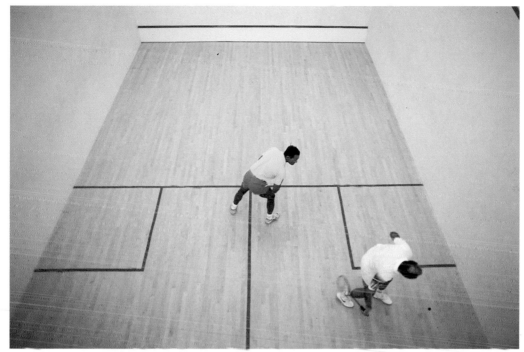

(a)

(b)

Figs 85 (a) and (b)   An early straight volley, when the server is slow to reach the T.

(a)

(b)

Figs 86 (a) and (b)   A wrong-footing crosscourt, when the server crowds the receiver.

(a)

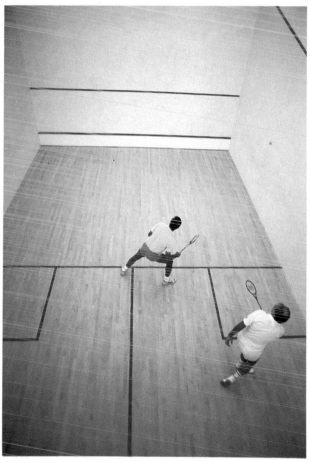

(b)

Figs 87 (a) and (b)   A straight drive, following loose front-court angle.

(a)

(b)

Figs 88 (a) and (b)   A deep crosscourt drive, following loose drop.

(a)

(b)

Attack your Opponent's Weaknesses

This is a factor that will have a very personal bearing on your choice of shots. The following are examples:

1.   *He is impatient.* So prolong the rallies. I know players who have set out with the avowed intention of 'boring the pants' off their opponents, hitting everything deep down the walls and never moving on to the attack. It is not the way I would wish to play a match, but against the impatient types, it does work.
2.   *He is a nervous starter.* So don't give him the chance to settle. Take the ball early and pour on the pressure. Volley whenever you can.
3.   *He is slow.* So look for an opportunity to play the moving shots, notably the boasts and the drops.
4.   *He is weak overhead.* So torment him with high lobs, especially close to the wall and on his backhand.

Defend your own Weaknesses

1.   *You are a nervous starter.* So give yourself a playing-in period, nothing risky. Just sticking to the basics. Straight drives down the wall, concentrating on length and width. As soon as you get your rhythm you will start to relax. Then you can bring in your full range of shots.
2.   *You cannot cope with the hard-hit ball.* So set out to break up your opponent's rhythm. Throw up some lobs. Don't give him any pace on which to work.
3.   *You are slow.* So don't give your opponent the chance to play short. Select shots such as the straight drive, crosscourt

Fig 89   Regard this shaded area as no man's land. Keep your own shots away from this area at all costs.

drive and lob which are targeted for the back corners. Only play the boast or drop when your opponent is badly out of position.

4.   *You are weak overhead.* Most lobs are played from the front quarter of the court, so again concentrate upon the back-corner shots.

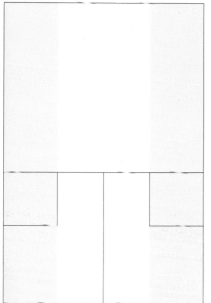

Fig 90 (a) Aim to play all your shots into the shaded area on either side of the court.

Fig 90 (b) This should be your ultimate ambition.

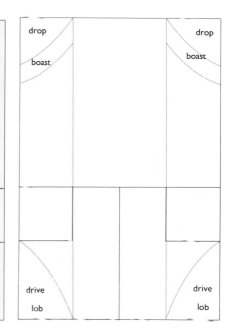

Fig 91 The ideal target areas for your various shots.

Never Drop from a Drop

This was Geoff Hunt's maxim, and like most of the things that Geoff said, it makes tactical sense. There is, however, a lesson to be learnt here. There are no absolutes in squash, no Holy Grail. Even the wisest advice can only be taken as a general guide.

Take this maxim. If your opponent has played a drop and is covering his own shot, it would be rash to reply with a drop of your own. However, if he was still moving back towards the T, a drop would be the right shot to play, because it would leave him hopelessly wrong-footed.

Look upon squash maxims as sensible guide-lines which can help to improve your correct choice of shot ratio. They will never be a total substitute for your finest ally: good, old fashioned common sense.

Summary

1. Set out to take your opponent's legs away.
2. Make him cover 'the maximum distance in the minimum time'.
3. Target the four corners.
4. Ideally, put the ball into the corner furthest from your opponent
5. Whenever possible, move him over the diagonal.
6. Attack your opponent's weaknesses.

STAR TIP

Never drop from a drop.
                              Geoff Hunt

KEY POINT

In squash, as in life, what was true yesterday is no longer true today. So if the drop that was working like a dream in your last match suddenly becomes a disaster, don't persevere with it. Analyse the problem when the game is over and solve it for tomorrow.

Use boasts and drops to move your opponent out of position, and only when you can regain the T position quickly.

7. Defend your own weaknesses.
8. Given the choice, play the shot that leaves you on the T.
9. Use lobs and floated boasts to buy time.
10. Don't forget the value of the unexpected.

CHAPTER 9

ALL IN THE MIND

A female admirer once commiserated with Nijinsky (the dancer, not the horse). She said, 'What a shame you can never see yourself dance'. 'Oh, but I do,' he replied, 'Always. I see myself dance from the outside'. It was the Russian's form of total concentration (his way of blotting out the world); and in his case, it had been achieved by a study of yoga.

This is a quality shared in differing ways by all of the great champions. Golfer Ben Hogan hurt the sensitivities of a friend by walking past him four times during a single round at Augusta without once acknowledging his presence. Afterwards the friend asked, 'Are you angry with me, Ben? Have I done something wrong?' And Hogan explained, 'When I play golf, I see only the ball'.

At squash, Jahangir concentrates so hard on court that he appears to have an almost mystic quality. If a firecracker exploded in the arena, he would be the last to jump. This is one of the reasons why he has remained at the top for so long. His temperament is so rock solid, his technique so firmly based, that he can produce a performance close to his best over and over again.

This has to be your aim too. Therefore, work on the positive factors that you need in your game: patience, concentration, determination, belief and, perhaps above all else, an inner calm.

Being Psyched-Up

There is a delicate balance between being psyched-up and being nervous. If you are properly psyched, the adrenalin will start to flow as soon as the game begins, and so will you. On the other hand, if you are nervous when you step on court, you will almost certainly start badly. The tenseness

of your body will make your shots tentative. Unforced errors will follow and, unless your opponent is similarly affected, you will soon be trailing. This will undermine your confidence still further and the chances are that you will eventually come off court knowing that you have not done yourself justice.

This is the story behind so many losing games. Most players new to competition find it easy to produce their true form in a friendly when there is nothing at stake, but put them in a match with a marker and even a scattering of spectators in the balcony, and all too often the rhythm goes away. Therefore, they give below-par performances on the days which matter most.

Of course, the aim of any competitor has to be that of raising his game on match days, whether leagues, ladders or tournaments. To achieve that aim, you need good mental preparation, involving essentially confidence and an inner calm.

Confidence

This must be built on solid foundations, so it is important to be able to prove to yourself that you are making steady progress by setting realistic goals. The leagues are obvious targets. If you are advancing up the leagues, however slowly, you are clearly improving. If one of your friends beats you 3–0; and then the following week, you lose to him again, but this time 3–1, it is still progress.

It is equally important to set yourself goals when practising, to see how many successive straight drives you can drop directly into the service box, how many successive volleys you can play from the short line, and so on. This is partly to make practice more enjoyable; partly to build

that confidence. Nothing is more likely to boost self belief than the knowledge that you have a sound basic game. With that behind you, you may still lose, but there will be no dark disasters.

Losing

Always try to win, but be philosophical about losing. Look upon defeats as nothing more than temporary setbacks. After all, you usually learn more from the ones you lose than those you win. To advance, you need to play people better than yourself, so defeats are inevitable.

It is important to handle such moments with a bit of style. Shake hands and say 'Well done' as though you mean it. Avoid the temptation to make excuses. Even if you genuinely believe you were a shade unlucky, don't say so. Examine the match with an honest mind and work out precisely why you came out second best. If you can do that, you will have gained something.

The British golfer Neil Coles caused an upset in the Ryder Cup by beating Cary Middlecoff on American soil. As the winning putt fell, Middlecoff reached out his hand and smiled. He said, 'You beat me on my very best day'. Now that was style — and not a bad example to follow.

Inner Calm

This is just as important to a squash player as confidence, but harder to find. It has to become part of one's lifestyle from the moment you rise in the morning until the time you hit the pillow at night.

There are several ways of achieving this. Jahangir attains his almost spiritual peace via Islam and prayer. Meditation does the

KEY POINT

The person who cannot control him or herself is unlikely to control a match. So develop a philosophy on court that remains shock-proof against natural disasters.

same for me. During some part of every day, I need to get away from the crowd, to think my own quiet thoughts and put things back into perspective. Then I too am at peace with my world, and nothing bar the odd earthquake will disturb me. Self-discipline, plus a willingness to face up to one's problems and solve them, will also help.

Muhammad Ali was once asked a hypothetical question: supposing he was awaiting the call to enter the ring to defend his title and he was told that his house had burnt down and his wife and children had died in the flames. What would he do? 'If that happened,' said Ali, 'I would still walk down that gangway to the ring and I would still win.' With Ali's strength of mind, he might well have done so too.

That is of course simply an extreme example of the need we have for tunnel vision when we move towards our chosen sporting arena. At such times, there can be no room for outside worries.

The Match Day

On the day of a match, arrive early, so that you can be relaxed and composed. If you are feeling tense, it often helps to lie full-length on a bench and then consciously relax each part of the body in turn. If you are still feeling nervous, remind yourself

Fig 92 Note the calmness of Umar Hyatt – a calmness undisturbed by the coming collision with Adrian Davies.

STAR TIP

Don't play on the day before a big match. To do your best, you must come on court, hungry like a lion before a meal.

Nasrullah Khan

that your opponent is quite possibly feeling the same way. It is also possible that he may not have read this book. In which case, the poor chap will be at a considerable disadvantage.

Try not to spend the 40 minutes prior to your game standing on the balcony, marking someone else's match. I know this can be a difficult situation when you are a member of a team, but avoid it if you can.

The Match

Use the knock-up to relax and regain any lost concentration. Get your rhythm going and study your opponent to see if you can discover any apparent weaknesses. Toss up a lob to see how sound he is overhead. Compare his backhand to his forehand. Is he really watching the ball? Is his footwork cumbersome? How does he handle the ball coming low off the wall? Can he cope with pace? This is all useful information for the match ahead. Moreover if you've been fully concentrating upon this task, the last vestiges of nervousness will have gone away.

Use a playing-in period to steady yourself still further. Be patient; no ambitious shots. Just rely upon good, basic length and let the other chap make the early mistakes. Those first few points are important psychologically. If lost, they can put doubts in the mind of a doubter.

Anger

Somewhere along the line, your patience will be sorely tested. Maybe you will meet a wind-up merchant who tries to unsettle

Fig 93   Jahangir questions a call in the British Open but, as ever, politely. Nothing is going to be allowed to ruffle that mystic calm.

you with talk; somebody who asks for too many lets; a marker who makes mistakes; or just a plain, old-fashioned cheat. We have a few of these but, fortunately, not too many.

I know that in a fast and furious sport such as squash, it is hard to stay calm in situations such as this, but for your own sake, it is important that you do. Otherwise your concentration will go and quite possibly the match too. By all means, feel anger but do not show it. Learn to channel it correctly and it will make you more determined than ever and, therefore, more likely to win.

If your opponent starts to argue with the marker, or throws a racket or whatever, don't get involved. This is a clear sign that the match is going your way. If you feel a bad decision has gone against you, by all means question it, but politely.

John McEnroe can explode, go to war with his opponent, the linesman, the umpire, the tournament referee and the crowd, and then win the next 6 points in a row; few others can. For the vast majority of us, outbursts on court are more likely to ruin our game.

Positive Thinking

While on court, allow only positive thoughts to run through your mind. We all make mistakes, but do not allow them to haunt you. The last rally is history, so do not dwell upon it. This is the prime reason why points so often go in runs as confidence ebbs and flows.

It is hard to maintain confidence, rhythm and touch throughout the entire course of a match, and this is a good thing to remember. Your opponent may have overwhelmed you in the opening two games, but the third is normally the hardest to win and he can so easily falter, so never give in. The history of squash is studded with tales of players who lost their concentration when the match was seemingly within their grasp.

In 1962, Abou Taleb was playing Mohibullah Khan in the final of the British Open. He was leading 8–1 in the fourth and serving for the match, just one point

The Reluctant Saviour

Gamal Awad, a nice but excitable little man, was bounding up the stairs with blood in his eye, as the saying goes. His quarry: the man who had just refereed his game. On the landing, he spotted Hiddy Jahan, and without so much a a by-your-leave, made a grab for Hiddy's racket. Hiddy held on to his famous Black Bat and for a moment the two men wrestled in silence. A David and Goliath contest, if ever there was. Then Hiddy enquired quite calmly, 'What are you up to, Gamal?' Awad glanced fiercely towards the referee. 'I'm going to hit that man on the head,' he said. Hiddy's own relationship with officialdom hasn't always been harmonious. And some detected a hint of regret as he shrugged and said, 'But not with my racket'.

away from being crowned the king of squash. However, Abou, being Abou, was not content to merely hit a winning shot. He wanted to lace it with magic, turn on the style. So he started rattling the tin and Mohibullah, playing the patient game, came back from the dead to win.

If that had happened to me, the memory would have stayed with me until my dying day. It may have haunted Abou, but if so he didn't let it show. He won the next three British Opens. To the best of my knowledge, he never made that mistake again.

Oddly enough his son Adam, who has inherited many of his father's touches, faced the same situation in reverse during a recent British Under-19 Championship. Two games down and 0–8 in the third, he decided that he had nothing to lose, so started to lob everything, and suddenly his opponent's confidence and rhythm had gone. Adam won quite comfortably in the fifth.

The scoring system in squash encourages such 'impossible dreams', because the player who loses his serve on match point will then have to win two rallies in a row, and with the pressure on, this can be tougher than it sounds. The advice to anyone on match point (or for that matter, anyone at 8 –8) is to play the pressurized basic game. To tell yourself, 'I'm just one shot away from victory', is a recipe for disaster. When it is tough, be patient and let the pressure tell on your opponent. In such cases, the game normally goes to the one with the most inner calm.

Weary Legs

When you are feeling tired and a bit desperate, always remind yourself that your opponent is probably equally tired and equally desperate, so do not encourage him. Develop a stone face. Smile through the pain. If you have to fetch the ball from the front of the court, breathe deeply while your back is towards him, then turn seemingly relaxed and easy. Seek to give the impression that you are much the fitter of the two. This can be devastating to the morale.

New Heights

Let us assume that you have achieved the perfect mental balance of total relaxation with total concentration. You are oblivious to everything outside those four white walls. Now at this point, with the adrenalin flowing, you may very easily gain your due reward and touch heights you have never known before. This is a phenomenon that many top sports players have encountered.

Many moons ago in the Bing Crosby Golf Classic, Ben Hogan needed an eagle three on the last hole to have any chance of winning. This was a dog-leg and if he played it the conventional way, there was no chance at all. Therefore, from an elevated tee, he drove straight across the bay and hit the fairway on the far side, chipped up and sank his putt. That was a carry of over 273m (300yd) across the sea.

During the shooting of *Follow the Sun*, the film story of his life, he was asked to repeat that shot. He proceeded to hit 100 balls into the sea. The situation was different and so he found it impossible to conjure up the magic again.

The majority of squash players can recount similar experiences. They will tell you with some wonder, 'I played out of my skin that night'. One of the most interesting examples came in the quarter-finals of the 1976 Pakistan Masters when Hiddy Jahan played the then reigning world champion, Qamar Zaman.

It was an emotional experience for Hiddy. During the previous two years, he had been banned from putting foot on Pakistan soil, unable even to attend his sister's funeral. Now the ban had been lifted and he was home again.

He had been a schoolmate and long-time friend of Zaman, but they had exchanged angry words at a recent tournament in Ireland. After beating Hiddy, Zaman had said, 'You're easy. I can beat you anytime I like'. Rash words when you are speaking to a man as proud as Hiddy. That proud spirit had been further affronted on Pakistan television when the interviewer had said to Hiddy, 'I presume this will be another Hunt–Zaman final?'

'Hang on a moment,' said Hiddy, 'Zaman has got to beat me first'.

'Umm, that's true,' replied the interviewer and shrugged for the benefit of the cameras, as though to suggest that this was little more than a formality.

Hiddy was still seething when he stepped on to court and what followed has gone down into the folklore of the game. Hiddy won 9–1, 9–3, 9–4 in just 29 minutes of the most thunderous squash anyone could remember.

Afterwards, the normally exuberant Zaman sat in the dressing-room as though shell-shocked. No one in the world could have lived with Hiddy on such a day. Rex Bellamy, the doyen of squash writers, has described it as the best squash he has ever seen, and clearly if Hiddy could have found the magic key to stay on that plateau, he would have been the game's long-time king.

The Gallway Theory

What is the secret of such days as Hiddy had? I like to believe that Tim Gallway has found the answer. Tim is the author of *The*

Inner Game (Jonathan Cape), a book that all serious squash players should read. The book is based on the notion that a player has two selves, which he calls 'Self 1' and 'Self 2'.

Self 1 is the thinking, logical part of the brain which gives instructions and criticizes you when you do not follow those instructions to the letter. Self 2 is the automatic pilot, the subconscious thought process of the brain. Gallway contends that we should try to free Self 2 from Self 1, giving the body the freedom it needs to take over and play naturally. You can look upon Self 1, if you like, as the negative part of our nature and Self 2 as the positive.

The problems come when Self 1 refuses to release Self 2 and continues to slip in those self-destructive, negative thoughts. Self 2 maybe goes for a winner and hits the rim of the tin. Self 1 introduces anger and self criticism. Unless Self 2 can swiftly reassert himself, the player may well lose the rallies that follow. With confidence and concentration denied, he is vulnerable.

However, it is no good going on to automatic pilot unless your game has first been built on sound foundations. For the Ben Hogans and the Hiddy's of this world, that is comparatively simple. Any shot they choose to play has, after all, been hit thousands of times in practice.

Tim Gallway's idea is that you programme Self 2 much in the same way that you programme a computer. He suggests that you do this by creating a series of mental pictures of what is required. You think about those images constantly until they are stored in the backrooms of your mind. Then if Self 1 can be banished, Self 2 will simply reproduce those pictures on court.

No one suggests it will come easily. You will have to work at it. This is where the friendlies are so useful. Always use them as the testing grounds for new ideas. At first, you will probably find that only the familiar bread-and-butter shots will arrive naturally –the straight drives, the occasional drop, and the lob when under pressure. However, keep on trying, because only good can be derived from this experiment. If nothing else, it will take you closer to that state of relaxed concentration which enables you to play to the best of your ability.

Remember, you cannot hit and think at the same time. Once you do that, the rhythm gocs.

All I can tell you for certain is that Gallway's theory has helped my own game. The magic moments are still too few and far between, but every now and then I hit heights which I once believed were beyond my reach. Whatever your standard, whatever your capability, I am quite sure it can help you too.

Summary

Before the Match

1.   Be psyched-up, but not nervous.
2.   Achieve inner calm in your everyday life.
3.   Build your confidence on solid foundations.
4.   A sound basic game is the best boost for self-belief.
5.   Work on the positive factors in your game.
6.   Remember that you learn more from the games you lose than those you win, so be philosophical.
7.   Seek to raise your game for the big days.
8.   Your overall aim is relaxed concentration.
9.   Arrive in good time for your match.
10.   Use the knock-up to relax.

During the Match

1.   When on court, learn to blot out the world.
2.   The last rally is history, so do not dwell upon it.
3.   Keep your cool. Do not get involved with temperamental opponents or one-eyed markers.
4.   Learn to channel anger, and use it to your own advantage.
5.   Develop a stone face when the going gets tough.
6.   When you are tired, remind yourself that your opponent will almost certainly be tired too.
7.   You cannot hit and think at the same time. Programme your mind, so that instinct can take over.
8.   Don't see the finishing line too soon.
9.   On the big points, be patient. Play the pressurized basic game, and let your opponent make the mistakes.

CHAPTER 10

INTO BATTLE

On the eve of the 1966 British Open, Jonah Barrington was in despair. He had trained for the tournament with a dedication hitherto unmatched in the annals of squash, forsaking the normal pleasures of the human race. Not for nothing was he known as 'The Monk of the West End'. Despite these sacrifices, he had been demolished by Azam Khan in straight games on six successive days.

Azam had retired from the tournament scene four years earlier following a succession of injuries and had not played competitive squash since, and yet Barrington, some twenty years his junior, still couldn't live with him. He decided to pull out of the Open.

Azam and Nasrullah would have none of this. 'Don't be silly,' said Azam. 'You do what I tell you, you win. You see what happens.' So Barrington went into battle with two of the best tacticians in the world in his corner.

In the quarter-finals, he was due to meet the defending champion, Abou Taleb, unbeaten for four years and the bookies' favourite, to retain his title. Azam's eagle eye had studied Abou and noted that although he moved well when taken to the front of the court, he was fractionally slow in returning to the T. Nasrullah, too, had noted the spreading waistline of the Egyptian. Abou had not been following the monastic ways of Jonah.

The advice from Azam was simple: 'Taleb play winner, you return winner. He play winner again, you return winner again. Taleb hit tin'. In other words, Barrington was being advised to play the patient game, to make his own fitness tell and eventually encourage Abou to destroy himself. History records that it worked. Barrington won in the fourth and moved on to eventually meet Aftab Jawaid in the final.

Now Jawaid was a very different type of player to Abou – a master of length, quiet, dignified, silky smooth and essentially orthodox. Most people would have said this was a man without any chinks in his armour. Barrington's cornermen disagreed. They were convinced that they had spotted a certain frailty in Jawaid's high backhand volley. Therefore, they encouraged Barrington to toss up a stream of high diagonal lobs to Jawaid's backhand, and sure enough the volleying of the Pakistani became steadily more vulnerable under pressure. Drop shots to both corners – another part of the master plan – completed the rout.

That Open underlined, as perhaps never before, the importance of tactics. Barrington, in both those key matches, was able to attack his opponents' weaknesses and to impose his own physical game upon them. This is, of course, an essential ingredient of any match plan. Set out with the intention of imposing your own tactics upon your opponent and of playing the game at the pace that suits you best.

Strengths and Weaknesses

Play to your strengths and defend your weaknesses, i.e. if the forehand drive is your strength, endeavour to play most of the game on that wall – tight with a mix of good and dying lengths. If mobility is your weakness, do not give your opponent the chance to play short, but do attack your opponent's weaknesses. For example, if he is impatient, prolong the rallies; if he is tense, play fast and hurry him into mistakes; if he is slow, play short and take him over the diagonal; if he is weak overhead, lob; if he is unfit, move him; if he is unimaginative, surprise him.

Courts

The British Open used to be staged at the Lansdowne Club just off London's Berkeley Square. The courts were subterranean and the heat unbelievable. Yellow dots behaved like blue dots, the ball was hard to kill and rallies consequently became long and tiring. It was claimed that home advantage was worth 3 points a game. Certainly strangers found it tough to say the least.

The advice to anyone playing at a rival club for the first time is to have a prolonged warm-up on one of the neighbouring courts before your match begins. If this proves impossible, use your 5 minutes knock-up time intelligently. Study the pace of the ball both off the floor and off the walls, notably off the back walls. No two courts behave in identical fashion and temperature has perhaps the biggest effect of all.

If the court is hot, the game becomes slower. The ball will be bouncing higher, so there is more time to play your shots. The ball will be coming easily off the back wall, as dying lengths will be hard to achieve.

Drops (unless directed into the nick) will be coming away from the side wall, sitting up and waiting to be hit. Rallies will be longer, because it will be harder to hit a winner, so you must be patient. Do not get frustrated and go for risky winners. Play to a good length and remember you can afford to be reasonably adventurous, because it will be easier to cover your own shots.

Hot courts can be tiring. Even with good ventilation, oxygen will be in short supply and you may be struggling for breath. Therefore, concentrate upon good movement and good shot selection. Ensure that your opponent does the running, moving him from front wall to back wall at every opportunity; while keeping your own movements to a minimum. On hot courts, games can become battles for survival with the spoils going to the strongest and the fittest.

Cold courts, by contrast, are boons for touch players. Drops and lobs will die fast and at the very least stretch your opponent, so you will be able to move him over greater distances. He will also need to run faster, as the ball will not bounce so high. Stun drives and kills are much more effective, and it is easier to achieve a dying length.

Good Habits

Most of us get our first taste of competition in club leagues, and work our way up as we improve. In those early days, victory all too often goes to the players who can hit hardest and run the fastest. Accuracy barely seems to matter at all. However, as you move up the leagues, things change. The shots which produced those early winners are being returned with ease. Those loose crosscourts are being intercepted in mid-court and driven deep, and suddenly you have become the chaser.

This is why it is so important to develop good habits from the very beginning. It may mean that progress will be slower, but it will be steadier and you will climb much higher. Squash is a rallying game and quick winners are rare. Therefore, learn to be patient and stop looking upon every shot you play as a potential winner. Concentrate upon good length and good width. Base your plan on a game that is safe from attack and yet puts pressure upon your opponent.

When you talk to men who have played Jahangir, they all say the same thing. He is so accurate, his shots so close to the wall, that he gives you nothing to attack. Eventually you are forced to gamble a little and that is when the errors arrive.

Sue Devoy follows much the same pattern. She is seldom spectacular in the opening game of a match. You will not see much of her feared backhand drop. However, she puts so much pressure

upon her opponents that many become ragged in the early stages of the second game. That is when the opportunities come and, from this point onwards, her drop shot will be used with ever greater frequency. The ideal moment to go for a winner comes when:

1.   Your opponent has hit a loose shot, been wrong-footed or is caught out of position.
2.   You can reach the ball in plenty of time with no need to snatch at your shot.

Rallying

This is such an essential part of squash that you need to be guided by good habits – simple rules which help you make the right decision.

1.   Concentrate upon good length and good width.
2.   Be patient.
3.   Make sure you can regain the T position after playing a shot.
4.   Don't play short when your opponent is on the T.
5.   Only play short when your opponent is behind you.
6.   Only play short if you can cover the shot.
7.   Don't give your opponent anything to attack.
8.   Make the four corners your target areas.
9.   Hit the ball as far away from your opponent as possible.
10.   Move your opponent up and down the court.
11.   Dominate the T.

Pace

Squash is full of one-paced players – players who go on court with the avowed aim of hitting the ball hard and low, hoping to blast their opponent off the court. The drive is often their only shot. They may be successful up to a point. They may win their club championships that way, but not, I fear, much else. For the variation of pace is an art that you need to master if you are to attain any real heights in the game.

KEY POINT

If you wish to reduce the pace for tactical reasons, learn to take the ball later, after the top of the bounce and from deeper positions in the court. Volley less, lob more. Stroke the ball rather than hit it.

You have to be able to slow the tempo down or speed it up, according to the state of the match. That decision will also be affected by your own condition and that of your opponent.

Squash can be oddly hypnotic at times. You can be faced by someone determined to take the cover off the ball and this is not your natural game, yet suddenly you find yourself trying to match him for power and pace, and in all probability losing out.

One of the key features of winning squash is that of ensuring that the game is played at the pace of your choosing and not that of your opponent. Therefore, if you are up against someone fast and

---

STAR TIP

The game may not always go to the man who makes his opponent run, but that's the way to bet.

Kevin Shawcross

---

furious whom you are finding it difficult to contain, don't give him any speed on the ball. Keep it tight and deep. Play a few high lobs to break up his rhythm. It is fairly simple to develop a good rhythm when every ball is sitting up knee-high. but once you have to play a few volleys above the shoulder, or a few tight boasts from the back corners, that rhythm may soon be broken.

See how he copes with the 'nothing' ball. A lot of hard-hitters find it difficult to generate any real pace off the softly struck ball that is almost too tired to bounce.

Up until now, we have been slowing the game down, but remember we have to vary this pace according to the ever-changing state of the match. Once your opponent begins to tire, you must increase the pace to make that tiredness tell. This does not mean that you need to hit the ball harder. You can speed things up by taking it earlier, hunting the ball, playing more volleys or by simply taking your opponent's time away.

Again do not wait for the big days before adopting this technique; perfect it in your friendlies, make it part and parcel of every game you play. And please do not become a one-pace player, as it can be awfully tedious.

Bounce

There is a lot of confusion over the point at which the ball should be struck. Some coaches advocate hitting it on the rise, others at the top of the bounce (at the moment when it hovers before gravity takes over) and some will tell you to hit it after it has started to fall. But that moment of impact is really determined by the shot you are planning to play.

If you are pouring on the pressure, going for pace, you will be happy to hit it on the rise. If you are going for a kill, you will wish to hit it at its highest point to avoid the danger of rattling tin. If you are playing a drop, you will want the ball to fall on to a nearly horizontal racket face.

There is a danger here of tangling up theory with reality. In an evenly balanced game, you will seldom be given the luxury of arriving with sufficient time to decide just where and when you are going to hit the ball. You just have to let instinct take over and, provided you have worked hard on your basic shots, your instinct will not let you down.

Buying Time

When striking the ball, you must always give yourself sufficient time to return to the T and thus cover the shot you have made. In some situations, this can be difficult.

Maybe you have been forced to scramble at the front of the court. You are off-balance and if your opponent can intercept your shot, you are going to be caught out of position. Therefore, hoist the high lob, and for safety's sake make it the

diagonal. By doing so, you will have bought yourself the time you need.

Maybe again, you are in trouble in the back corner and being forced to boast. Your opponent is aware of your lack of options and he is also fast around the court. You fear the quick drop before you can fully regain position. Therefore, play a floated boast that will take longer to arrive. True, he will get to it even more easily, but by then you will at least be back in position.

Remember, do not trail your racket head. Run with it in the ready position. That saves time too.

Mistakes

In his early tournament days, Hashim Khan played most of his shots above the cut line, because he was so anxious to avoid the danger of hitting tin. This sounds strange when you realize you are talking about so great a player. It underlines the dislike top players have of making the two most basic mistakes: hitting tin and serving out.

As the tin is only 48cm (19in) high and the out-of-court line on the front wall is 5.7m (15ft) above the floor, it does seem amazing that the tin is rattled so frequently.

STAR TIP

The front wall is a high wall. Why waste it?

Qamar Zaman

Unforced errors have more to do with the winning and the losing of matches than the spectacular shots which linger in the mind. Whether a ball strikes the wall a few centimetres above the tin or 15cm (6in) above is usually incidental, so learn to play within your limits. Experiment, but be realistic and always allow a margin of error.

If you look upon that 30cm (1ft) above the tin as your target area and one shot in every four is going down, you will clearly have to raise your sights. One out of ten just might be acceptable, but this would really depend upon the fate of those other

nine. If six of them were creating winners, there would be no need for change. That would be just a question of playing the percentage game.

The same thing applies to a lob serve. It would be nice to hit the side wall a few centimetres beneath the out-of-court line over and over again, but even the champions would not be that ambitious. The risk far outweighs any possible gain. Therefore, again set your own limits, and err on the side of caution.

The T-Area

The T is so named, because it forms the junction between the short line and the half-court line. Many players, advised to take up position on the T, will stand on the short line with their feet planted on either side of the half-court line, convinced that they are following instructions to the letter. However, as you will see from Fig 11, the T is really an area which surrounds the junction, and the position you take up in this area will depend very much on the state of the rally.

Most top players today prefer to stand about a metre behind the short line. But if speed is not one of your strong points, you would be wise to move forward on to the short line itself.

If you are able to anticipate the next shot, it would be sensible to adjust your position accordingly.

Let's say, for instance, that you have your opponent in deep trouble in the backhand corner, and that he only has one option – the boast. Then you could quite reasonably move forward into the front forehand area of the T with the intention of putting him into further trouble by playing a quick drop.

Alternatively, maybe the match has developed into a long series of drives down the backhand wall. As the non-striker, it might be a good idea to stay on the left-hand side of the T-area, looking for an opportunity to cut off one of your opponent's drives.

However, always be prepared for the unexpected. So long as you stay within that area, you will still be able to cope.

Fig 94   A classic lob from Adrian Davies. Note how low he gets.

A friend of mine plays an underarm scoop from behind the short line which drops neatly into the front corners. It is not a shot that I would recommend to my pupils, but he plays it with such ease and accuracy that it wins him a lot of points. Of course, its very unorthodoxy helps, as it is hard to read, particularly when you are meeting him for the first time.

Tactical Balance

This is largely about *when: when* do I attack; *when* do I defend; *when* do I play the pressure game; *when* do I stroke for pace; *when* do I stroke for position?

The right choice of options may well prove to be the difference between the winning and the losing. Start your match and every rally with defence. Be patient. Set out to force openings before you move on to the attack.

> **KEY POINT**
>
> Don't try to win the point too soon. If you attack the good ball, you will make too many errors. Remember, patience is one of the greatest squash virtues.

If defensive shots are loosely defined as back-corner shots, and attacking shots as front-corner shots, a suitable balance between the two may be 75 per cent defensive and 25 per cent attacking. Keep your game simple: defence first, then pressure and positional play to create openings, and attack to finish.

A Game Plan

In 1981, Toronto staged an historic match: the World Open final between the reigning champion Geoff Hunt and the young pretender Jahangir Khan. It was the end of a great reign and the beginning of another. Hunt was thirty-four and Jahangir seventeen, so the battle plan of Rhamat (Jahangir's coach and mentor) was predictable enough – the young legs would be made to prevail.

The importance of the T position is twofold:

1.   It is the point closest to all four corners and, therefore, the point which gives you the best chance of reaching all your opponent's shots.
2.   It enables you to intercept any ball passing through the centre of the court; and therefore provides plenty of opportunities for a good volleyer.

Remember the player who commands the T normally wins.

An Unorthodox Game

Squash would be a very boring game if we slavishly followed every dictum from the coaching manuals, so never worry if part of your game is unorthodox, just so long as it works for you. Half-volleys, for instance, are not recommended in many manuals, but they can nevertheless become a very useful surprise shot when played well. Indeed there are times when you are caught with the ball at your feet when they become the only shot available.

Although the plan was simple, the execution was brilliant and could serve as a blueprint for your own game. Rhamat told Jahangir not to worry about who won the first game. The important thing was to keep the Australian on court for as long as possible. Therefore, Jahangir, at his most defensive, made the back corners his targets. The rallies were long, the drives tight and relentless.

After 40 minutes, Hunt eventually took that opening game. But by then Rhamat and Jahangir were confident that their plan would succeed. And so it proved.

In the second game, Jahangir turned on the pressure, taking the ball early, hunting for it, volleying, giving a tiring Hunt no respite. Every time the return was weak (if only fractionally), Jahangir would switch to the attack with a mix of drops, front-court angles and volleys into the nick.

These are the basic copybook tactics. When playing defensively, endeavour to keep the ball tight and in the back corners; take command of the T and try not to make mistakes. However, if the mistakes continue, fall back on to basics until you have regained your confidence. Also, have a very sensible margin of error. It is a big wall out there in front of you, so there is no excuse for rattling the tin.

Remember to always look for the opportunity to pressurize your opponent by taking his time away – taking the ball early, upping the pace, mingling good lengths and widths with the dying, volleying and pressure driving.

Attack the ball that is 'on', i.e. an easy one, and attack when your opponent is out of position. Of course, this is an interchanging situation. You will be pressurized too and under attack, so always be prepared to switch back to the defensive game.

Flexibility

There is a danger of coming on to court with a game plan that is too rigid and then failing to change it. For instance, the chap you were told was slow turns out to be Carl Lewis in disguise. Therefore, all those short shots which were going to destroy him need to be revised hastily. Impressions from the knock-up can also send you off down the wrong trail. It is not unheard of for an accomplished volleyer to mishit a couple of overheads during the knock-up, just to encourage his opponent to feed his favourite shot during the match itself.

There are two simple rules which it is wise to follow: firstly, *don't* change a winning game – you have the tactical balance right, so don't spoil it; secondly, *do* change a losing game.

Summary

1. Set out to impose your own game upon your opponent.
2. Endeavour to see that the match is played at the pace that suits you best.
3. Hot courts can be tiring, so move well and conserve energy.
4. Remember drops and lobs die fast on cold courts.
5. Base your plan on a game that is safe from attack, yet still pressurizes your opponent.
6. Don't become a one-pace player.
7. Don't become a one-shot player.
8. Mistakes lose matches, so eliminate the unforced errors.
9. Play within your limits.
10. The T is an area, not a set spot, so do not become static.
11. Remember that the player who commands the T normally wins.
12. If an unorthodox shot works for you – use it.
13. Start every rally with defence.
14. Break up a hard-hitting game with lobs and the 'nothing' ball.
15. We have a big front wall, so learn to use it all. Height is the third dimension and much under-used.
16. Be selective, and only attack the ball that's 'on'.

THE ADMIRABLE CRIME

I have been fortunate enough to have rubbed shoulders with many of the giants of the game. I have admired the bravery and the dedication of Jonah Barrington, a man who made the 'impossible dream' come true; I admired the mental strength of Geoff Hunt, a Churchillian fight-and-fight-again man; and I have a lot of respect for Jahangir Khan who may well be the best squash player of all time – anyone capable of remaining unbeaten for five years and seven months in a game played on the razor edge has to be a bit special.

However, the five men who have done most to fire my imagination are Hashim Khan, his brother Azam, Abou Taleb, Qamar Zaman and Hiddy Jahan, because they played squash the way I believe it was meant to be played – adventurous, imaginative, colourful stuff, and something to be enjoyed by spectator and player alike.

I was too young to see either Hashim or Azam in their prime, but even in their declining years, I found them wonderful to watch. I played Azam when he was nearly fifty and even then his volley drop was as good as any I had ever seen. Abou was just Abou, a man whose racket became a magic wand. Zaman was a bewildering entertainer who could baffle the best, while Hiddy can be thunderous and silky smooth all in the same rally.

Needless to say, all five were masters of deception – the admirable crime.

The whole basis of deception is to show your opponent the shot you are shaping to play and then, at the very last moment, play something else. It is a fascinating branch of squash and therein lies the danger. Players can so easily become obsessed with it to the exclusion of all else, and then its value has gone. If you overdo deception, it loses its element of surprise and ceases to deceive.

When Will I See You Again?

In 1971, the Australian ladies team led by the legendary Heather McKay were playing in Karachi. Pakistan squash is totally male dominated and there were no changing facilities for women at the club. So they changed in a spare room, which was guarded on the outside by a fiercely handsome young man, a warrior-type who captured the girls' imagination. They eventually said goodbye to him with some regret, convinced that they would never see him again. They were wrong. Three years later, they came to England and watched him play in the British Open. His name was Torsam Khan, older brother to Jahangir.

In other words, the more often you play the basic percentage shot, lulling your opponent into a false sense of security, the more effective deception is likely to be.

Maybe you have hit five successive straight drives from a position just in front of the short line. Now, from a similar position, you are shaping to hit a sixth, but almost on the point of impact, you change the pace and the angle of the racket face, and the shot perhaps becomes a straight drop, gentle boast or deep crosscourt.

I have known players so anxious to get the balance right that they hit their shots to a ratio of 6 to 1 – six basic shots followed by the false one. It did not take their opponents long to guess when the next bit of deception was due. So remember: if you wish to deceive, do not be predictable.

Feet, Body and Head

When using deception, you simply take up the correct position for the shot you are shaping to play. Your body and feet thus aid the deception. One of the reasons why Zaman is so bewildering lies in his footwork. This would horrify many conventional coaches, because it barely exists and, therefore, provides no clues at all. Anyone playing Zaman would be well advised to totally ignore the feet and the body of the man, as they will lead you astray.

Ignore the head as well. One of his favourite ploys is to shape up for a crosscourt drive. Then, at the moment of impact, his head will turn to look back over his shoulder as though following the flight of the ball. Meantime the ball is heading straight down the side wall. The best advice you can give to anyone facing such a man is to focus your eyes on the ball, the racket face and the wrist. Even the wrist (as you will read in a moment) can mislead.

The Backswing

If you are planning to mould deception into your normal game, it is wise to use the same backswing for every shot.

Delay

This is a key element in deception. The idea is to reach the ball early with your racket in the raised and ready position. You feint as though to start the downward swing, stop, hold the shot, then play the

---

STAR TIP

Accuracy is more important than violence.

Gogi Alauddin

Fig 95   Which way will the wrist turn this time? Qamar Zaman, also a master of deception, watches the wrist and racket of Hiddy Jahan.

ball. That delay, however brief, will hopefully have forced your opponent to commit himself. At the very least, it will have created a moment of uncertainty. Either way, you have achieved the first part of your aim.

The Wrist

The use of the wrist is another key element, and Hiddy Jahan is the great master of this technique. Off a short ball (using the same swing), he can caress a drop or crack a drive, simply with a flick of the wrist. Or again, he will shape for a drop, sense his opponent coming fast up the diagonal and then, at the last possible moment, his wrist will turn and a hard, low crosscourt will leave that opponent for dead.

Jahangir also makes good use of the wrist. From the front of the court, he will shape to drive and then turn the wrist, so that the ball is hit gently into the side wall and becomes a trickle boast; or, maybe from just in front of the short line, he will again shape for a drive and then suddenly

hit a crosscourt heavily cut past an unbalanced opponent.

Masking

Another useful aid to deception is the masking of the ball with your body. This means that your opponent will not see the moment of contact and so will be forced to move late to cover. However, be careful not to stand on the shot. As soon as you have played the ball, move away, so that your opponent can have a clear path to it. Masking unfortunately leads to a lot of let calls mostly from people who don't really understand the rules, for it is a perfectly legitimate tactic and an important one to master.

> **KEY POINT**
>
> If you have a shot you can disguise better than any other, don't squander it. Save it for the moments when points are particularly precious.

Wrong-Footing

Every now and then you will come up aginst someone who is so fast around the court, such a good retriever, that they will be reaching every shot you play, bar the odd nick. Therefore, to win, you will need to wrong-foot him.

We will assume that in addition to being quick, he also positions well, taking up a nicely balanced stance on the T. Now as long as he has the time to take up that position, he is going to be difficult to wrong-foot, so we need to take that time away by putting on the pressure, making our basic shots more searching, volleying and making sure that we get to the ball a little earlier than before. He will now be finding it harder to regain the T, and this is where the opportunity to wrong-foot him will come.

The normal methods of deception – the use of delay, wrist and masking – will serve this purpose. Every now and then when he is caught out of position, play the ball back

Fig 96   The wrong-footer. Hiddy Jahan has shaped to play a crosscourt and then at the last moment, his wrist has turned to drive the ball down the forehand wall. Ian Robinson smiles in acknowledgement.

to the point from which he has just hit it. For example, suppose he has hit a loose crosscourt from the front right-hand corner which you can intercept and volley. Meanwhile he is still on the move, heading back towards the T. Then I suggest your target has to be that front right-hand corner, the position he is leaving at speed.

Practice

It is not wise to become too involved with deception, until you have mastered the basics. However, there are certain elements you can introduce from a very early stage. For instance, learn to look upon the drop as a dummy drive. This can be introduced neatly into a pairs practice routine, with one player boasting from the back court and the other straight driving. However, every once in a while, the drive

---

> **KEY POINT**
>
> The trickle boast is essentially a surprise shot, and most effective when used sparingly, thus heightening the element of surprise.

---

becomes a drop. The success rate of this deception is based upon the number of drops reached by the playing partner.

You can also introduce the surprise crosscourt into the same routine – the ball being hit in the basic side-on stance with the front foot and head facing the side wall. The only proviso is that (if these are early days) you should also practise hitting the crosscourt with the feet in the correct open-stance position.

When teaching the art of deception to my pupils, I explain to them that when

Fig 98

Fig 97   Rodney Martin in position to play a wide range of options against compatriot Chris Robertson.

Figs 99 (a)–(i)   The nine options from a front right-hand corner position.

Figs 99 (a)–(i)   Remember that your opponent mustn't know which of the nine options you are choosing until contact has been made. Therefore, it is vital to adopt the same basic stance with the racket at the top of the backswing (as in Fig 98) when playing each of these shots.

(a)   The straight drive to length.

(b)   The stun drive.

(c)   The crosscourt drive.

(d)   The straight lob.

(e)   The crosscourt lob.

(f)   The straight drop.

(g)   The crosscourt drop.

(h)   The trickle boast.

(i)   The reverse angle.

picking up a loose return from a position in the front right-hand side of the court, they have nine options, and that their opponent should never know which option they have chosen until the shot has been played.

The nine options are: the straight drive, the crosscourt drive, the straight lob, the crosscourt lob, the straight drop, the crosscourt drop, the trickle boast, the reverse angle, and the stun drive.

On this exercise, all these shots are played as though for a straight drive with a full backswing. I then switch on my ball machine and encourage them to run through the full range of those shots over and over again, but not in any sequence – just as the spirit moves them. If your club does not possess a ball machine, persuade a friend to boast rather loosely or alternatively to straight feed you from the short line.

Deception should be regarded as an important part of the squash technique, but never as an isolated art. If you can blend it into your game, you will become a much better player. You will find that it can be a great equalizer. If you really work at it, you will soon be able to play on level terms against many of those who outgunned you in days gone by. Equally important is the fact that it will add much pleasure to your squash.

Summary

1.   Don't overdo deception, as it will cease to surprise.
2.   Your deception will be only as good as your basic game.
3.   Use the same backswing for every shot.
4.   Delay is the key to good deception.
5.   Use the feet, body and head to confuse.
6.   When masking, remember always to clear your shot.
7.   When wishing to wrong-foot someone, first take away their time.
8.   Avoid the danger of becoming predictable.
9.   Learn to use the full repertoire of shots.
10.   One of the secrets of deception is getting to the ball early.

Fig 100   The delayed shot. The ideal set-up for deception. The downswing has been checked momentarily by 'holding' a shot in this way, one sets out to wrong-foot the opponent.

KEY POINT

Deception is an art first learnt painstakingly on the practice court, then introduced gently into friendlies, and finally used sparingly in match play.

PART 4

PATH TO PERFECTION

CHAPTER 12

IMPROVING YOUR GAME

Gary Player had just played the most remarkable recovery shot from the depths of a bunker. The ball had climbed almost vertically above the flag, bitten with the backspin and stopped within 45cm (18in) of the hole. The South African had just touched the peak of his black cap to acknowledge the applause when his playing partner commented, 'You were a bit lucky there, Gary'. Player, fortunately a polite man, let the silence drag out and then he mused, 'It's a funny thing. But the more I practise the luckier I seem to become'.

It was nicely done. It is a remark that could apply to all sports, but notably squash. When you see a top professional play a crosscourt volley into the nick, don't imagine that this was a hit-or-miss shot or that too much luck was involved. Chances are that he or she had worked on that shot for countless lonely hours in a bid to achieve the perfection that is beyond the reach of us all. It is one of the ironies of squash that top players practise continuously; the duffers just play.

If your only court time is spent playing matches, you will improve up to a certain point, but eventually you will be stranded on a plateau from which there is seemingly no way up. If you wish to make steady progress, you must practise regularly. Book a practice court for at least one session a week and then there are no real limits to how good you can become.

What to Improve

Work on your weaknesses, not on your strengths. Most players, in the early stages at least, are stronger on the forehand. So concentrate on your backhand. Make it every bit as strong as your forehand, and that improvement alone could advance you a couple of leagues.

If the return of serve is posing problems, then you probably need to concentrate on volley practice. If the back corners are proving to be something of a nightmare, then work on your defensive boast, and so on. But don't complicate things; be content to concentrate on one shot at a time.

Building on Basics

Whatever you do, do not ignore the basics. Otherwise you will be in the same situation as a student who has never mastered simple division, suddenly being confronted by complicated mathematical problems.

I know there is a temptation to go on court and practise the corkscrew serve, the skid boast and the most spectacular volley nicks – the Bobby Dazzler shots – but get the basics right first. The pillars of your game are ball control and racket control, correct movement and positioning. Until you master these, you have nothing to build on, and any advance in your game will perforce be very minimal.

There is a saying that 'Perfect practice makes perfect'. In other words, to get the full benefit from practice, quality must be your watchword. Don't be casual, don't skimp and don't cheat on either the swing or the movements; you will only be cheating yourself.

Practice can be Fun

One of the reasons people are so reluctant to practise is that they consider it a bit boring – certainly not as enjoyable as a competitive game – but it doesn't have to be that way.

If you are going to practise solo, set yourself targets. See how many straight drives out of twenty you can drop into the service box, how many continuous volleys you can hit from behind the short line, and so on. Constantly try to improve your own records. Then you will know you are getting better.

Find a practice partner (equally anxious to improve) and try out the pairs routines. Play the condition games (described at the end of this chapter) and make these as competitive as you wish.

Play Regularly

If you wish to improve, it is vital to play regularly, at least once a week, preferably more often. If you are in a club, join the leagues and enter competitions. Play friendlies against as many different opponents as possible. Play slightly better players who will stretch you. Play slightly weaker players who (in friendlies at least) will provide the opportunity to try out the crosscourt lob you practised so assiduously last night. Don't make the mistake of playing the same person all the time, as you will both wind up with very limited techniques.

STAR TIP

Anyone can be good player, if they wish. Practise your weak shot. Go on court by yourself for an hour every day and hit, hit, hit. You soon be good player.
                                    Nasrullah Khan

Coaching

This book provides a self-teaching programme. It cannot, however, analyse your individual needs the way a coach can. Therefore, if you have the opportunity for some coaching, take it. A good coach will be able to spot flaws in your technique of which you were blissfully unaware. You go to a doctor for the occasional medical check-up; let a coach check out your game.

Solo Practice

Solo practice can improve your ball control and technique. It can also improve your shots and the accuracy and consistency of these shots, namely your skills.

Firstly concentrate on technique, secondly on placement and thirdly, where appropriate, on pace. Don't forget to work on both forehand and backhand in the following exercises.

Service box drives (above the cut line) Drive the ball into the service box and concentrate on this as a target area. See if you can hit twenty continuously behind the short line or ten continuously into the box. Initially, make things easy for yourself. Come out a bit from the side wall and hand feed the ball at the start of the rally. Make the drives tighter as you progress.

Service box drives (below the cut line) This is the same exercise as above. Only this time you will need to hit the ball harder to get the depth.

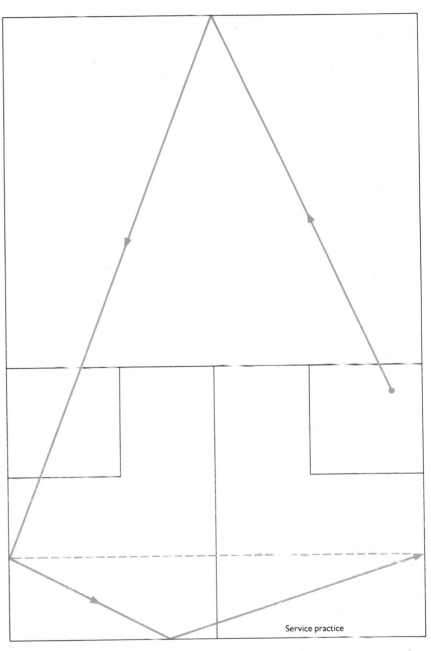

Fig 101   A service practice to test your accuracy. If played correctly, the ball should reach the forehand side wall before recrossing the dotted line – 1.5m (4ft) from the back wall. Place a spare racket on the court floor as a check mark.

Length drives   This time, the target area will be just behind the service box. It is good practice to alternate between above and below the cut line. Take the ball off the back wall.

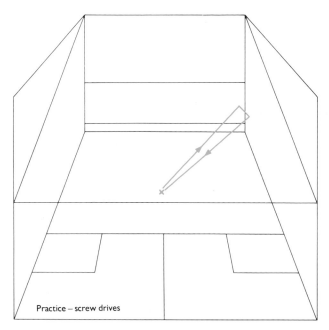

Fig 102   Screwdrives. The forehand front-side continuously.

Fig 103   Corner screws. (a) The forehand crosscourt (front-side). (b) The backhand crosscourt (front-side).

Length drives and boast   Drive three times and then boast. See if you can get the second bounce to die in the nick.

Straight volleys   Build up your volleys in the same way as the drives, giving yourself targets at each stage. Start at the front and gradually work your way back until you are volleying behind the short line.

Feeding and drops   Hit a couple of drives to warm up the ball, then feed with a soft shot to the front (maybe a gentle boast) and drop.

Corner exercise   This is a front-corner exercise that helps you get used to angles. Hit a forehand (front/side) to rebound into the middle, followed by a backhand (front/side) into the opposite corner, and so on. See how many you can hit continuously. Play your shots close into the corner, otherwise you will lose control of the rally.

Corner exercise and drop   Feed backhand crosscourt (front/side) and drop. Then repeat with a forehand crosscourt.

Volley corner exercise   This is a repeat of the corner exercise, only this time you volley and all the shots are played above the cut line. See how many you can hit continuously.

Alternate volley exercise   Volley alternately, forehand and backhand. Start half-way between the short line and the front, then gradually move back behind the short line. Once again, remember to set your own records.

> **KEY POINT**
>
> When solo training, set specific targets. For instance, how many successive volleys can you hit on to the front wall? Create your own record today and beat it tomorrow, then again on each succeeding day. This brings two bonuses:
>
> 1.   It makes the practice enjoyable.
> 2.   It gives you visible proof of the fact that you are improving.

> **KEY POINT**
>
> Concentrate on quality practice. Behave as though you are in a match situation. Once your shots become slapdash, stop and call it a day. Twenty minutes of quality practice is worth an hour spent casually knocking the ball around a court.

Pairs Practice

Pairs practice is the next step after solo practice. It allows you to practise technique, a greater range of shots, movement and working under pressure.

Hitting across   This is how we normally knock-up, but it is also an excellent way to practise. The intersection of the short line and service box provides a useful target. Make an easy start, hitting soft and high.

Feeding (from behind) and driving   Player A drives from a position half-way between the short line and front

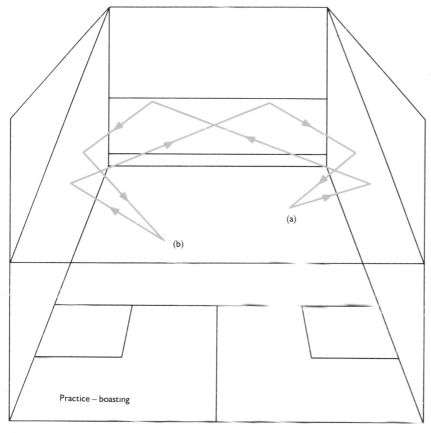

Fig 104   Boasting. (a) Backhand boasting. (b) Forehand boasting.

wall. Player B feeds from just behind the short line, making sure that the ball bounces well in front of his partner. This should be continuous, not a stop-start routine.

Boast and drive   Straight drives for length. B boasts. A repeats the drive on the opposite wall. B boasts and so on.

Boast, drop and drive   B boasts from the back corner. A plays a drop and then a drive. B boasts and so on.

Drop and crosscourt; straight drive and boast   A two-shot exercise. A drops and then crosscourts. B straight drives and then boasts. Concentrate on controlling the shots, but don't beat yourself.

Boast and crosscourt   From the front. A crosscourts. B boasts.

Volleying across   A repeat of the hitting across exercise, only this time, A and B volley to one another from the short line.

Drive and volley boast   Another version of the boast and drive exercise. A straight drives. B plays a volley boast from the short line.

Feeding (in front) and drop   From the middle of the court, B hits a forehand into the corner (front/side) to rebound into the middle. A (moving from the T) plays a drop into the other corner. B hits a backhand into the same corner (front/side) and A drops into the opposite corner.

Circling   Both A and B drive straight off the back wall (aiming above the cut line) and circle via the back wall to the half-court line and then the T.

Condition Games

Condition games provide practice at specific shots and combinations in a game situation. They can also be used to equalize players of different standards. The stronger player can be bound by the rules of the condition game, while the weaker is allowed to play a normal game.

High game   The ball can only be played above the cut line. The first player to hit below loses the point.

Back game   A game played in the back of the court, behind the short line.

Front game   A game played in front of the short line.

Front/back game   A has to play all his shots into the front half of the court (a very attacking game). B has to play all his shots into the back of the court.

Volley crosscourt game   A has the right back half of the court, B the left. They volley across to each other, winning points when they land the ball in their opponent's area.

Back game with crosscourt rule   Play a game just using the area behind the short line. You can play any shot to this area, but crosscourts must hit the side wall, or you lose the point.

Back game and drops   A defensive game played in the back half of the court. But this time one attacking shot – the drop – is allowed.

Back game and boast   The same game as above, only this time the attacking boast replaces the drop.

Middle game   A game played between the short line and the front quarter of the court. This is good practice for front-corner shots.

Side game   A game played within the width of the service box, using the full length of the court, but only one side. This is perhaps the most important of all condition games . . . the base upon which all good squash is played.

Summary

1.   Practise at least once a week.
2.   Work on your weaknesses, not your strengths.
3.   Keep it simple. Concentrate on basics at first.
4.   Remember: 'Perfect practice makes perfect'.
5.   Let quality be your watchword.
6.   Devise ways of making practice enjoyable.
7.   Set yourself solo targets.
8.   Seek out a practice partner.
9.   Play regularly with different opponents.
10.   Have some contact with a coach.

Figs 105 (a)–(f)   Practice areas for condition games.

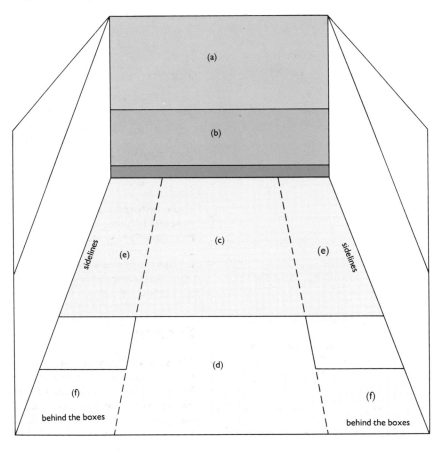

(a)   The top half of the front wall, the area above cut line, is ideal for encouraging good length.

(b)   The bottom half of the front wall, the area below cut line, is ideal for concentrating upon attacking shots.

(c)   The front half of the court, the area in front of the short line, is ideal for playing a game of drop shots.

(d)   The back half of the court, the area behind short line, is ideal – when combined with the area in Fig 105 (a) – for encouraging good length.

(e)   The sidelines (left and right), the area within the serivce box width and stretching the entire length of the court, is ideal for improving width.

(f)   The back corners, the area behind the service boxes and within their width, is ideal for encouraging good length and good width.

CHAPTER 13

FITNESS AND PREPARATION

The day in 1966 when Jonah Barrington became the British Open champion proved to be a watershed for the sport. Champions set the style and Barrington – a spartan and fitness fanatic – was a very different proposition from the champions who had gone before.

Hashim Khan contended that the best way to get fit for squash was to play squash. His stamina was legendary. He once played continuously for nine hours. However, the open country and the gyms were not for Hashim. His brother Azam shared the same philosophy and once claimed he could not run, not even for a bus.

The Egyptian Abou Taleb, a magical man, was genuinely astonished to learn that his young challenger Barrington had forsaken drink and women. That wasn't Taleb's style at all. If it had been, Barrington would doubtless have been forced to wait a little longer before taking over the crown.

Once champion, Jonah set a standard for fitness that has been followed by top players ever since. His methods were daunting to say the least. He ran cross-country in the company of international athletes. He pumped iron. He worked out in gyms for hours at a time. He even tried to run up a mountain.

If you wish to become a good squash player, you would be wise to follow at least a little way down the same path – but give the mountain a miss.

Squash is a physically demanding sport, because there are so few respites during the course of a game. Therefore, you do need to be fit. However, fitness is only one of the qualities you need, so don't go overboard. True, it would be sad to develop outstanding racket skills and then

fail time and time again, because your legs had turned to jelly, but it would be equally sad to become one of the fittest fellows in the universe and then fail, because you had never really learnt how to swing a racket. So strike a sensible balance between the two.

A Fitness Programme

Any fitness programme needs to concentrate upon four major needs: speed, stamina, strength and agility. As

---

KEY POINT

Begin any fitness programme gently and patiently. Build progressively, a little more each week. This will benefit you by:

1. Reducing the risk of stiffness and pulled muscles.
2. Ensuring that you don't put too much pressure on the heart.
3. Making you more conscious of the ever-growing sense of well-being that fitness brings.

---

with your court skills, be patient. Do not expect to be transformed overnight. It is no good, for example, going flat out for a week before an important match. This will simply weaken you. Six to eight weeks would be a reasonable time-span for a fitness build-up to produce encouraging results. It might also be wise to put the emphasis on stamina and strength during the off-season, and technique and tactics during the season.

Energy

Firstly, it is important to understand the two main sources of energy used in squash.

Aerobic

The heart and lungs provide oxygen for the muscles. This energy system is called aerobic (meaning 'with air'). It is normally created by continuous activity (20 minutes or more) which raises the heart-rate.

Anaerobic

This is the term for energy that is in the muscles which, when overworked, causes muscular fatigue (wobbly legs). Anaerobic training involves short bursts of work followed by rest. This is called interval training and includes short sprints on a track, or shuttle runs on a court.

Running

This is the most common exercise used to create aerobic energy. If you have not run for a while, start gently. For the first week, run and walk in alternate stages. Maybe use telegraph poles, lamp-posts or trees as marker posts. In the second week, run and jog in alternate stages. And in the third week, turn the exercise into a continuous

---

KIT CHECK

Insoles Sorbathane insoles will help absorb shock. Spenco insoles will help prevent blisters.

run. Gradually build up the pace and length of your run to at least a minimum of 20 minutes. Then try to reduce your time over a set course.

Shuttles

This is one of the best forms of anaerobic exercise, and involves short bursts of sprinting followed by periods of rest. Start with six sets of 30 seconds, running lengths of a squash court. Gradually build up to ten sets and then build up the times to one minute. To make the exercise doubly valuable, fit in various squash movements such as running backwards, sideways and lunging.

Circuit Training

This type of training is unique in that it combines both muscular and cardio-vascular fitness. It consists of a number of exercises (eight, ten or twelve) using the main muscle groups in turn. Emphasis is placed on the groups used in squash.

Each exercise is performed in quick succession and this can be done either at home or on a squash court. Test yourself by doing each exercise for one minute. Gradually build up to three circuits. The endurance aspect of the circuit can be increased if an aerobic exercise is performed after each circuit exercise. Running on the spot, or astride jumping twenty times, followed by five squat jumps, is ideal.

Circuit exercises

Running on the spot Do this fast, lifting your knees as high as possible.
Press-ups From the knees.
Alternate leg thrusts While crouching, kick each leg out behind you in turn.
Back arch While lying on your stomach, with arms outstretched, lift your arms, head and chest.
Side bends Reach down sideways and try to get your hand over your knee.
Sit-ups While lying on back, with your feet flat and knees bent, lift only your head, shoulders and arms and touch the top of your knee.
Trunk twists With your arms in front, turn to each side in turn.
Squat Keeping your back straight, bend your knees until your thighs are parallel with the floor.

The Warm-Up

By the time you walk on to court, you need to be thoroughly warmed-up, loosened, stretched and prepared to make full use of the knock-up to follow.

There are four parts to your warm-up:

1. A warming exercise, e.g. jogging and limbering.
2. A loosening or mobilizing exercise.
3. Stretching exercises. Hold each stretch in position where you feel a slight 'pull'. Count slowly to ten. Do each stretch at least three times.
4. Practising your strokes as you would wish to use them in a game.

Try the following routine:

Warming

1. 100 jogging steps.
2. 50 astride jumps.
3. 50 punch-ups.
4. 50 front strides.
5. Continue a little, jogging and skipping through the loosening and stretching exercises.

Loosening 'Top to Toe'

Sky reach With your arm straight overhead, reach as high as possible and hold, alternating sides. Do ten repetitions.

Head circling Turn your head to the left, then to the right, push back and forward. Repeat ten times. Circle slowly four times each way.

Shoulder shrugs Bring your right shoulder up to your ear and hold. Do ten repetitions. Repeat on the left.

Arm circling Do this forwards and backwards, ten of each.

Arm flings Push your arms back, towards each other behind your body. Repeat this ten times.

Trunk twists With your arms straight in front, turn them and your trunk to the side as far as possible. Repeat ten times each side.

Side bends With your arms at each side, bend sideways and reach down to touch below your knee. Do ten each side.

Trunk circling With feet astride, bend down and touch your right foot, swing across to the left, swing up and over in line with shoulders and repeat. Do ten each way.

Hip circling With your hands on your hips, thrust your pelvis forward, side, back, side. Ten times each way.

Ankle circling Do ten full circles in and ten out, for each foot.

Stretching

Lunge or hip flexor stretch Stand with one leg in front of the other, bend to a lunge position and straighten the back leg as much as possible. Hold. Repeat on the other leg.

Abductor stretch Turn sideways from your lunge. With the toes of your stretched leg facing forward and your foot parallel to the ground, the thigh abductors are stretched. If the toes are turned upwards, the inner hamstrings are also stretched. Hold.

Quadriceps stretch Standing on one leg, clasp the ankle of your free leg and raise the leg gently backwards with knee bent, arching back. Hold.

Hamstring stretch Sitting on the floor with your legs outstretched, clasp your toes and press your trunk and head gently down toward your legs. Hold.

Calf stretch   Bend one knee and stretch the other leg straight out behind, keeping your heel on the ground and your knee straight. Hold.

Grooving

A little shadow practice before you go on court will help you to ensure that you are thoroughly warmed-up, and allow you to start concentrating on your strokes. Start thinking your way into the match.

Summary for all the Chapters

The following are some squash sayings that may help:

1.   The player with the stronger basic game usually wins.
2.   Don't run to the ball. Move to the place you want to hit the ball from.
3.   The walls don't move, so watch the ball.
4.   Exert maximum pressure with minimum risk.
5   Your last shot is history, so concentrate on the next.
6.   Perfect practice makes perfect.
7.   If you find a situation difficult, the chances are your opponent will too. So!
8.   Don't change a winning game. Do change a losing game.
9.   Play the ball where your opponent isn't.
10.   Play to your strengths. Defend your weaknesses.

A Final Word

During the winter of 1987, I staged the World Invitation at Bromley Town and so came into contact with Zarak Jahan Khan for the first time. He was nineteen and being hailed as Pakistan's latest rising star. It was easy to see why. He was quite simply the fastest thing I had ever seen on a squash court. Dead nicks apart, he appeared capable of getting absolutely everything back.

Equally impressive to me was his training programme. Zarak would rise at 5 a.m. each day and go for an 8-mile run. The rest of the morning would be shared between the running track and squash court. He would spend the afternoons in the gym and the evenings once more on court. He would eventually return home at nine, have his supper and be in bed by ten.

Even by the exacting standards of the professional squash player, this was a remarkable example of dedication. And with big brother Hiddy as his coach and mentor, he soon began to justify all that early promise.

I signed him as lead player in my American Express team and had good reason to be glad that I had done so. He went through his first season unbeaten. He reached the position of ninth in the world and was still climbing. That very knowledgable man, Mohamed Dadir, prophesized that within a few years Zarak would be jostling with Jansher Khan and Rodney Martin for the world's number one spot.

Then on a dark day in Stuttgart, he snapped the cruciate ligaments at the back of his knee. That, to most people, seemed to be the end for Zarak. Few players who have suffered such an injury ever play again. None have ever returned to scale the heights.

The trouble was that no one had told Zarak this. As soon as he could walk again,

---

KEY POINT

Set yourself on-going targets, instead of limits, for the great beauty of squash is that you will keep on improving, just so long as you have the necessary desire and dedication.

---

the training resumed, gently at first, but building up in intensity week by week. He began to play competitively only to discover that speed, the great jewel in his crown, had faded. He was being beaten by men who couldn't have lived with him in days gone by.

However, supported by Hiddy, he fought on. He returned to that demanding training routine which had first taken him towards the top; and slowly the knee was mending and the speed returning. Now, at the time of writing, he is once more climbing the rankings. Against all the odds, the prophesy of Dadir could well come true.

STAR TIP

For all the good things in life, there is a price to pay. And in squash terms, this means that if you wish to reach the top, you must pay with total dedication and hard toil. There is no easy road.

Hiddy Jahan

That is the sort of dedication needed by a man who wishes to go all the way in this game of ours. I am not suggesting for a moment that you attempt to emulate his training programme. You doubtless have work to do during the daytime, family commitments and so on.

But I do suggest that you use Zarak as an example to follow. Because dedication is the quality in squash that separates the men from the boys, the women from the girls.

A coach can guide you along the way, improve your technique and tactics. But in the final analysis, it is down to you. If you really want to improve and transform your performances, you can – just provided you are prepared to listen and learn and work at your game.

I hope very much that you do, and wish you well.

INDEX